ECONOMIC DEVELOPMENT POLICY

with emphasis on Viet-Nam

R. W. Lindholm

School of Business Administration
University of Oregon

D1472257

ECONOMIC DEVELOPMENT POLICY

with emphasis on Viet-Nam

R. W. Lindholm

Dean, School of Business Administration
University of Oregon

School of Business Administration
Fiftieth Anniversary Publication Series

Cover by Dennis McBreen
Set in Ronaldson Linotype
Printed on Simpson Eggshell Text

UNIVERSITY OF OREGON PRESS
EUGENE, OREGON
1964

LIBRARY HOLDINGS AT   <Press F13 to see other locations>
1.   LOCATION: Earlham -- Lilly -- CALL NUMBER: HD82 .L48

<Searching: Library Catalog -- Holdings Display>

Find...   Options...   Locations Backup Startover Quit Help...

AUTHOR: Lindholm, Richard Wadsworth, 1914-

TITLE: Economic development policy with emphasis on Viet-Nam
       [by] R. W. Lindholm.

PUBLISHED: [Eugene] School of Business Administration [University

-∨

Enter any word or combination of words -- AUTHOR, TITLE, SUBJECT,
PUBLISHER, etc. -- and press RETURN. Press F10 to cancel.

LIBRARY HOLDINGS AT   <Press F13 to see other locations>
1. LOCATION: Earlham -- Lilly -- CALL NUMBER: HD82 .L48
    STATUS: Available

Type a number for more detail, or press NEXT for more information.

Bureau of Business Research Studies

1. TAXATION AND CONSERVATION OF PRIVATELY OWNED TIMBER. Wesley C. Ballaine, editor. 1959. $2.00.
2. ELECTRIC UTILITY NON-USER BENEFITS FROM OREGON HIGHWAYS. H. T. Koplin and D. A. Watson. 1959. $1.00.
3. THE PROBLEM OF THE UNINSURED MOTORIST IN OREGON. Raymond C. Rauch, 1959. $1.00.
4. OBSTACLES TO RAILROAD UNIFICATION. Roy J. Sampson. 1960. $1.00.
5. THE IMPORTANCE OF INTERNATIONAL TRADE TO OREGON. James N. Tattersall. 1961. $2.00.
6. RAILROAD SHIPMENTS AND RATES FROM THE PACIFIC NORTHWEST. Roy J. Sampson. 1961. $2.00.
7. CHANGES IN OREGON EMPLOYMENT, 1947-1960. Donald A. Watson. 1962. $2.00.
8. INSURANCE MANAGEMENT PROBLEMS OF SMALL RETAILERS. Donald A. Watson and A. Gerlof Homan. 1962. $2.00.
9. PUBLIC LIBRARIES IN OREGON. Mary E. Phillips and Catherine Lauris. 1962. $3.00.
10. RISK MANAGEMENT IN A CATASTROPHE. Mark R. Greene. 1963. $1.00.
11. A FORECAST OF THE FOREST RESOURCE AND INDUSTRY OF DOUGLAS AND LANE COUNTIES. Louis Hamill. 1963. $2.00.
12. RAILROAD SHIPMENTS AND RATES INTO THE PACIFIC NORTHWEST. Roy J. Sampson. 1963. $2.00.
13. OREGON HOUSING FACT BOOK. Clyde E. Browning. 1963. $2.00.

ANNUAL PUBLICATIONS

OREGON ECONOMIC STATISTICS. Jeannette Lund, editor. $2.00.

Business Administration Occasional Papers

THE STUDY OF ADMINISTRATION. E. W. Wengert, Dale Harwood, Jr., Lucian Marquis, and Keith Goldhammer. 1961. $2.00.

THE OREGON ADVISORY GROUP IN KOREA, 1959-1961. A report on the University of Oregon Mission to the Korean Economic Development Council. 1961. $2.00.

JUDGMENT, FACTS, AND THE CONATIVE DECISION IN ADMINISTRATIVE ENTERPRISE. W. Dwaine Richins. 1963. $1.00.

School of Business Administration Fiftieth Anniversary Publication Series

SELECTIONS FROM THE OREGON BUSINESS REVIEW, 1941-1964. Catherine Lauris, editor. 1963. $2.00.

BOARDS OF DIRECTORS: STRUCTURE AND PERFORMANCE. Stanley C. Vance. 1964. $4.00.

ECONOMIC DEVELOPMENT POLICY, WITH EMPHASIS ON VIET-NAM. R. W. Lindholm. 1964. $4.50.

Other titles in preparation.

The preceding publications may be ordered from the Bureau of Business Research, Room 361, Commonwealth Hall, University of Oregon, Eugene, Oregon.

Preface

The lectures and articles of Professor Richard W. Lindholm gathered in this book provide an insight into the problems faced by the economic advisors of low-per-capita-income countries. Professor Lindholm speaks from considerable first-hand experience gained in Pakistan, where he was a Fulbright Fellow in 1952; in South Viet-Nam, where he was a consultant on economic development for ICA from 1955 to 1957; and in Korea, where he was Coordinator for the University of Oregon Advisory Mission from 1959 to 1961.

The selections in Part I deal with general problems of development that must be solved by all emerging nations. Parts II, III, and IV more specifically refer to problems encountered in Pakistan, Korea, and South Viet-Nam. However, many of these problems are also common to other developing areas. Finally, Part V tells a few of the organizational and administrative difficulties encountered by advisors to nations trying to improve production methods and increase per capita incomes.

Recent events in Asia, Africa, and Latin America make clear the shortcomings of our economic development efforts in the past. Professor Lindholm's experiences can provide an insight into our errors and suggest recommendations for future policies.

Arthur S. Flemming
President,
University of Oregon

Contents

Part I

GENERAL ASPECTS
OF ECONOMIC DEVELOPMENT
POLICY

Accelerated Development With a Minimum of Foreign Aid and Economic Controls

This article is reprinted with permission from Social and Economic Studies, March 1960 issue, which is published at the University College of the West Indies in Jamaica.

Professor Lindholm sets up a model of economic growth that includes as a basic assumption falling prices in the developing country relative to world price levels. This is a well-considered challenge to the proposition, more popular a few years ago than today, that a government of such a country may hasten its economic development by increasing the means of purchasing through its fiscal and monetary policies.

Lettered references in the footnotes refer to the bibliography at the conclusion of this paper.

This paper considers a policy presented as an answer to the question: Would it be possible to reduce economic controls and need for foreign government aid in free underdeveloped countries without decreasing, and perhaps increasing, the rate of development?

The policy selected for testing is entirely a domestic policy of the underdeveloped country. It consists of three interrelated parts:

1. A money supply increasing less rapidly than productivity passing through the market place; i.e., falling prices.[1]

---

[1] Price stability is considered a neutral monetary policy which is not enough to satisfy the ends of a country in a hurry which wishes to utilize completely every type of help available. To support the position that price stability actually means neutral money, i.e., that money exerts neither a positive nor a negative influence, I can only refer to the vast amount of economic theory that has assumed prices to be constant and has therefore considered value in real terms, which means that these theorists have gone behind the veil of prices in order to isolate

2. An active government bearing a considerable portion of the burden of investment in power, transportation, education, and the like; i.e., in social capital and primary industries.[2]

3. A tax program with a minimum price push impact, which causes a minimum siphoning off of profits; i.e., land and gross receipts taxes.[3]

This policy would accelerate development through expansion of investment. The way in which it would take place is based on three groups of assumptions:

A. Privately controlled businesses and individuals will generally be able to undertake attempts at maximizing their well-being within the framework provided by 1) government economic leadership activities and 2) shifts in prices and earnings as established relatively freely in the market place. The major exception to reliance on signals in the market place is that government will follow a general economic development program that will frequently vary from market-established priorities. This group of assumptions also includes a government that 3) does not throw roadblocks in the way of private economic efforts.

B. It is also assumed that productive investment in a low-per-capita-income country seeking economic modernization is dependent upon elements quite different from those dominant in capital-rich, democratic-capitalistic countries, such as the United States and Canada. The principal productive investment determinants in the type of

the problems to be considered and "assume out" the effect of changes in the value of money.

In this paper, inflation is considered a destructive monetary policy and quite unacceptable. This position cannot be developed at this time, and I must rely upon reference to authoritative statements. For example, Eugene R. Black, President of the International Bank for Reconstruction and Development, stated at the 1955 Annual Meeting that "Economic expansion can all too easily bring about monetary inflation that is fundamentally the enemy of economic development, and in too many countries unwise economic policy has allowed it to do so."

When referring to the relation of inflation to economic development, Norman S. Buchanan and Howard S. Ellis write (A—listed at conclusion of this paper) : "It may therefore be necessary for foreign lending authorities to refuse to lend without stipulations concerning the achievement of balanced budgets, restraint of credit, and so on, unless they are prepared to see the economic fruition of their loans destroyed by inflation and adverse foreign balances in the borrowing country."

[2] In the words of Everett E. Hagen (E), "In Japan, the Soviet Union, China, and India, the favorable event was the coming into power of a government eager to aid the transition."

[3] The rapid industrial development of Puerto Rico has been particularly closely related to tax policy.

country considered in this paper are assumed to be 1) the ability of the government and other would-be domestic investors in
productive capacity to commandeer domestic economic resources and
2) the net inflow of capital from foreign countries.[4]

C. Because a program of the type being tested must rely heavily
upon the signals of the market place, a final assumption must be made
that government policy and public attitudes are basically pro-competi-
tion and anti-monopoly.

It is a positive program which does not dim the market signals, provides for government investment leadership, and is helpful in facilitating B-1 and B-2.

When B-1 and B-2 are considered largely on the basis of their monetary and fiscal elements and the basic policy stated above, the following
principal action concepts develop—first, in relation to commandeer-
ing of economic resources by domestic government and private resources:

1. The government must be able to gain control over economic resources a) without the necessity of applying
   high tax rates that are difficult to administer and always discourage individual initiative[5] (policy point 3)
   and b) without the use of inflation, with all its well-
   recognized attendant difficulties[6] (policy point 1).

2. It must be possible for the government and private
   individuals to sell securities, primarily of the debt type,
   to domestic savers and/or institutions holding savings[7]
   (policy point 2 and assumption B-1).

3. Private investors in secondary and tertiary industries must enjoy a maximum benefit from a correct estimate of market trends and the introduction of efficient production procedures[8] (policy point 3 and assumptions A-2 and A-3).

---

[4] C. G. F. Simkin (U) emphasizes the close relationship of the inflow of
foreign capital to economic development.

[5] Ursula K. Hicks (H) points out that "on economic grounds a reduction in
the taxation of profits should have a high priority if additional investment is
needed."

[6] Also, the 1955 Annual Report of ECAFE (Y) warns "that deficit financing
might properly be used by government . . . but that such a policy should be
adopted with extreme caution lest inflation, with all its undesirable social and
economic consequences, should result."

[7] Professor Howard S. Ellis (A) puts the point this way: "For any government, but especially for the government of rapidly developing countries, a broad
and receptive market for government bonds with the saving public affords an
invaluable, indeed an almost indispensable, basis for domestic finance without
inflation."

[8] Basically this assumption requires governments to resist the temptation to

—and second, in relation to inflow of foreign investment:

1. The cost of living must be kept down so that wage levels permit low production costs in relation to average world costs[9] (policy points 2 and 3 and assumption B-2).

2. Taxes on profits must be considerably below those prevailing in developed countries[10] (policy point 3 and assumption B-2).

3. Easy repatriation of earnings must be assured[11] (assumptions A-3 and B-2).

The remainder of this paper will be devoted to demonstrating that the goal, the policy, and the assumptions constitute a realistic program possessing a high degree of economic inner consistency and feasibility.[12]

The first policy point provides for conditions leading to falling domestic prices. Also, monetary and fiscal conditions consistent with this policy stimulate the type of activity assumed in B-1 and B-2. This economic relationship is to a considerable extent fundamental to answering the question posed in the first paragraph and is, therefore, legitimately considered first.[13]

---

increase tax collections from the most profitable or to permit labor to increase substantially wage payments in this sector of the economy. Also, governments must resist pressures for a rapidly expanding social security program.

[9] In Puerto Rico, where industrial development has been very rapid, the average weekly earnings in manufacturing establishments has risen from $18.18 in 1947 to $28.90 in 1957. In the United States, average weekly earnings of workers in manufacturing establishments in 1957 were $82.80. The mechanization in Puerto Rico manufacturing plants is frequently as modern as that existing in the United States and sometimes more modern.

[10] It appears that profits necessary to attract foreign outside investment to a country as well situated as Puerto Rico must be in the neighborhood of 30 per cent.

[11] Business people continually emphasize the desirability of converting foreign currencies. Of course, some sort of a guarantee of convertibility is necessary if foreign private investment is to be made. *Newsweek* (R), in an article entitled "What Worries the Overseas Investor Most," lists as the fourth greatest cause of worry: "Currency problems, including restriction on the right to withdraw earnings from the country or even to get back the original investment." This same situation was found in a U. S. Department of Commerce study (Y).

[12] Some may also consider the analysis to provide support for the political workability or unworkability of the policy selected for testing. This is not the purpose of the analysis and any conclusions of this type must be read into the study.

[13] David Felix (D), in a careful consideration of the impact of inflation on profit margins in underdeveloped areas, as evidenced by available Western European data during the 16th, 17th, and 18th centuries, and some current analyses, is able to conclude that: "Profit inflation does not appear to have been a

Expansion of Productive Investment
with Falling Prices

The use of a monetary and fiscal program consistent with the policy being tested, plus assumptions introduced, causes the findings of conventional monetary analysis to be reversed. An increase of the desire for liquidity and a reduction of consumption expenditures become a stimulant of productive investment rather than a deterrent; and the possible deterrent to investment in commerce and real estate of falling profits through falling prices acts as a method of channeling monetary savings *into* necessary social capital and primary industries and generally *out of* trading and capital holdings economically feasible only because of anticipated price increases.

A program of investment in social capital and primary industries financed by the government can be financed out of domestic voluntary savings only if savers are willing to purchase government securities. Savers will not purchase government securities of the conventional type under conditions of inflation.[14] Gimmicks to change this relationship are not likely to be helpful.

Savings made when prices are declining are best used to purchase government bonds or kept in bank accounts and savings institutions. Savings used this way gain purchasing power and earn interest. But savings invested in things would only retain purchasing power, and savings held as cash would not earn interest. Also, interest rates will fall because they need not compensate for rising prices. This will cause outstanding securities to rise above par, making possible new offerings of government or private securities at a lower interest rate, with every likelihood that the new securities will be eagerly sought.

It follows also that as the government's investment program begins to yield results, the power and transportation facilities and training institutions will be expanded and improved. In the type of situation under consideration, the lack of these facilities seems to frequently be a greater deterrent to the expansion of production than a shortage of markets and in many instances even the shortage of capital.[15]

This shift in the flow of savings will, of course, cause a large

---

major industrial stimulus either in the salad days of European industrialization or in newly industrializing countries today."

[14] "Only a few Brazilian states or municipalities have the opportunity of financing expenditures in excess of revenues without direct recourse to bank credit, since the market for fixed interest obligations, including federal government bonds, has been weakened by the long inflation to such a degree that long-term bonds are not bought on a voluntary basis" (I).

[15] This point is self-evident. C. N. Vakil and P. R. Brahmanand (Z) are generally opposed to large-scale basic investment by the Indian government, but they do recognize the need for government action to provide external economies, which is, after all, a large portion of what is being considered here.

portion of the downward pressure on prices provided for in policy point 1. This effect is to be expected because of the expansion of the supply of goods on the market without an equivalent expansion of the money supply or the velocity of money. The impact will differ from that under previous price and policy conditions because investment will bring forth a constant stream of saleables, and therefore each turnover of purchasing power encounters additional goods and services in the market place. This, of course, is much less the situation when the expenditure of savings is made in a way that best protects the economic position of persons under conditions of constant or rising prices.[16]

Also, downward price pressures of the type included in policy point 1 can be confidently expected as a result of increased monetization of the economy as it progresses.

Government Investment Expenditures

In the discussion of falling prices (policy point 1), it was necessary also to consider the role of government investment (policy point 2). Here, where the major emphasis is on government investment, it will also be necessary to refer to the other policy points.

Falling prices have been considered to be anathema to economic development.[17] Government investment expenditures are very important in preventing this development under the policy being tested.

Falling prices are usually expected to cause a reduction of economic activity because they:

● Increase the desire to hold money or assets stated in money terms and reduce the desire to hold things, and this—

● Decreases expenditures, particularly of the investment type, below income of the previous period, which in turn—

● Causes economic stagnation, unemployment, and a reduced national income.[18]

Sometimes the reason for the reduced production effect of falling prices is stated as a result of falling real and money profits arising from the stickiness of money wage rates. More often the argument is stated in the reverse as a principal basis for the stimulating im-

---

[16] ". . . the weakness of the market incentive for private investment . . . may help in some degree to account for the common observation that such domestic saving as does take place in underdeveloped countries tends to be used unproductively: hoarded, exported, or put into real estate" (S).

[17] In 1933, when there were 13 million unemployed in the United States, wholesale prices were 33 per cent lower than in 1929 when the nation enjoyed prosperity.

[18] This is based on the development of this subject in Hansen's *Business Cycles and National Income* (G).

pact on production to be expected from inflation (rising prices due to demand pull).[19]

The task of showing why falling prices, if experienced under the conditions of the type being examined, will hasten economic development is surprisingly simple and really involves the change of only one of the assumptions used when falling prices and economic stagnation are considered as two sides of the same coin. The assumption is that falling prices reduce the total of real expenditures; or when stated in terms of profits, that a fall of profits causes reduced investment and therefore unutilized savings. In the economic setting in which this analysis is developed, all the forces arising from falling prices (that are assumed to exist when the forecast is for economic stagnation, including that of falling money profits in the traditional profit areas of the type of economy under discussion) remain operative. However, the expectation is not economic stagnation because the impact of falling prices does not cause a drop of total real expenditures; instead, it provides the basis for an increase of real investment expenditures of the type which expands production, and this expansion of investment expenditures absorbs all resources released through the impact of falling prices.[20]

Deflation is very helpful to a government seeking domestic savings to support public investment. It causes a desirable redirection of the savings flow while avoiding the use of administrative devices. The impact also strengthens democratic-capitalistic institutional arrangements and encourages the inflow of capital from foreign sources.

The savings flow induced by deflation is 1) an answer to the argument that printing press money (deficit finance) or very high taxes are needed if the government is to gain control of the resources required for economic development. By accomplishing the end of government control of resources without controls or high taxes, a general

---

[19] This is the theme that W. Arthur Lewis uses constantly in developing "a case for inflation in currently underdeveloped countries." Professor Lewis is so entranced with the logic of the position he develops to show that a government's use of an expanded money supply to stimulate investment increases the total investment within a low-per-capita-income nation, that he is quite impatient with case studies which reveal the reverse effect. For example, he states: "In recent literature some naïve investigators have professed to show that inflation does not increase capital formation by showing that in a number of places where inflation has occurred (notably in Latin America) capital formation has not increased" (K).

[20] More than likely the factual relationship between falling prices and investment needs more exploration. For example, during the short period "from 1893 to 1896 the price level in Great Britain fell 45 per cent, in Germany 41 per cent, in France 43 per cent, and in the United States 39 per cent" (L). Also, U. U. Nef (Q) points out that the thesis of E. J. Hamilton (F) and J. M. Keynes (J) that the fall in real wages was a prime cause of industrial development in Great Britain cannot be accepted.

price decline is 2) an answer to the pleas for additional technical personnel to administer an economic control program, for certainly the purpose of an economic control program is to avoid the injustices and disruption caused by the inflation arising from the government's expansion of the money supply.

Under conditions of falling domestic prices (policy point 1), savings, for reasons mentioned above, flow readily into government securities; and the quantity of savings is increased because postponement of private spending is encouraged, for future cost expectations are below current costs.

In the countries under consideration, persons with savings have been very prone to use them to purchase land, gold, inventories, or to make investments abroad.[21] The continuing basic reason for this has been the desire to preserve the purchasing power of their savings. Under falling prices this basic reason is eliminated, and the traditional uses of savings become unattractive.

It would seem that one important impact of this change would be the development of pressures for expanded agricultural production, because investment in idle or partially idle agricultural land would lose its profitableness. Another impact would be to make merchandising and investment in luxury apartment buildings less attractive. Both of these impacts and others that could be mentioned, such as increased generality of the purchasing power of the domestic monetary unit which the reduction of controls would provide, would increase the drawing power of the high profits that have been available all along in manufacturing. These shifts would be intensified by the tax program of policy point 3.

If the pressures arising from policy point 1 and assumptions A-2, A-3, and B-1 are correct and the above relationships appeared, the result would be expansion of investment in production without the accompanying disruption, injustice, and economic waste involved in administering government economic controls and higher rates of taxation.[22]

Private Domestic Investment Expenditures

Under the policy selected for testing in this paper, private productive investment is stimulated in four major ways: 1) the reduction of savings flow through falling prices (policy point 1), 2) the provision of primary and social capital (policy point 2), 3) the reduction of

---

[21] See footnote 16.

[22] James E. Meade (N) in writing about economic controls in Great Britain says: "To give central and local officials the daily task of handing out, on what must inevitably be to a large extent arbitrary considerations, pieces of paper called permits or licenses of great value to the fortunate but limited number of recipients is to expose our fine and honourable public service to a strain which may in the end prove unbearable."

taxes on profits (policy point 3), and 4) inducements to foreign private investment arising from all three policy points.

The tax program (policy point 3) is particularly important in its relationships to private investment. It was shown that the selected policy points 1 and 2 would channel savings and investment toward productive uses. Policy point 3 is of particular assistance in stimulating a more productive use of land resources. However, policy point 3 has additional important functions.

For example, the lower tax on profits increases the return to the domestic private investor and would compensate somewhat for downward tendencies likely to arise from policy point 1. To the foreign investor the reduction of taxes on profits would provide a greater net gain because then he would be less concerned with the domestic deflation. Therefore, the combined effect is to stimulate private investment. It would also be true that this type of a tax structure permits profit margins to do a more effective job of allocating investment resources.

A final and related consideration concerning policy point 3 is that it keeps profits in the hands of the people who have demonstrated a capacity to operate a profitable enterprise and a willingness to assume the risk that is so important in this use of funds.[23]

In the writing, theorizing, and "research" related to accelerated economic development of low-per-capita-income countries, two broad schools of thought have developed. The one which has been most influential, particularly where government economic leadership is accepted to be important, has considered high taxes as a desirable method of making savings (tax collections in excess of current expenditures) available for investment. The other school of thought has seen high taxes as discouraging investment through the reduction of incentives to assume investment risks and to make consumer purchases.[24]

Although the possibility of collecting taxes in excess of normal budgetary requirements and using the excess to finance government investment in new productive enterprises has had a theoretical appeal, its actual implementation has not been the rule.[25] The usual

---

[23] Mr. Robert L. Garner, President of the International Finance Corporation, in his address to the Second Annual Meeting of the Board of Governors of the International Finance Corporation (New Delhi, India, 8 October 1958), said: "The successful businessman everywhere is accustomed to taking a chance, of risking his efforts and capital to take advantage of an opportunity to build his business and make a profit. Therefore, he responds most to those elements which make the opportunity more alluring and increase the possibilities of profit."

[24] The program of accelerated development advanced in this analysis would belong in "spontaneous order" of the dichotomy including also "deliberate order" (T).

[25] This is the situation to be expected when per capita annual incomes are likely to be around $100 and when the normal operations of government are so incompletely provided. In addition, the powerful feudal groups frequently control

reason for the failure in implementation has undoubtedly been the difficulty of raising the quantities of tax revenues required except under
conditions of a very productive foreign exploitation of a national resource; this, for example, has been the basic reason for the ability
of the tax program in Iraq and Venezuela to finance investment. But
even under these very favorable conditions, the political and economic
impact has been somewhat less than good.

All too frequently tax revenues have not been sufficient to finance
regular government expenditure, to say nothing of desired government
investment activity. Under these conditions, the outcome has usually
been budgetary deficits, with the borrowings made possible through
an expanded money supply.[26]

Another consideration reducing the desirability of using tax collections in the type of situation under consideration is that the high tax-
paying businesses often possess a monopoly position. It is understandable, if taxes must provide savings under these conditions, that governments might encourage monopoly, or at least not actively discourage it (violation of assumption C).

Private Foreign Investment Expenditure

Whether or not the policy being examined will provide an important stimulus to foreign investment must be a significant aspect of
whether it is a desirable policy for an underdeveloped country seeking
acceleration of its speed of development. It would seem that all three
points of the policy combine to provide a very considerable stimulus.

For example, policy point 1 (falling domestic prices) would be
very helpful because it would make investment attractive prior to the
development of an adequate domestic market. Making this possible
is an important step in breaking through one of the circles of despair
encountered in economic development literature.

The circle is of this sort: 1) Industrial development in a low-per-
capita-income country is restricted because the domestic market for
the products to be produced is inadequate. 2) A sufficient number of
people with incomes adequate to buy the production is not possible
until industrial development has provided productive work opportunities and the higher incomes that go with these opportunities. 3)

---

the government directly and/or indirectly. A. R. Burns (B) makes a comment
relative to this point when he writes: "Taxes on land or the income from it . . .
are often low, and such taxes have provided a declining proportion of all (underdeveloped) government income since 1938."

[26] Edward S. Mason (M) does not develop the point of failure of efforts to
raise taxes greater than normal government expenditures, but he does raise the
question of "whether this task lies within the capacity of democratic governments."

Therefore, industrial development is impossible in relatively small and low-per-capita-income countries.[27]

Because large quantities of unemployed savings do not exist in the world today, investment from abroad is not likely to be forthcoming unless there is a considerable profit inducement.[28] Low cost of production is one very important way to assure these necessary large profits. In addition, the rate at which profits are taxed affects the profits available for distribution to foreign investors. Under most circumstances the use of taxes to provide investment funds from the government budget will be self-defeating; the tax rate will have to be so high that it will either force up domestic prices or remove the profit incentive to continue operations and expansion.

There is also another aspect of the policy being tested which impinges very directly upon the attractiveness of the country to foreign investors. This has to do with the usefulness of the overall program in providing assurance to foreign investors that earnings may be repatriated and that they will not encounter foreign exchange problems in the purchase of equipment and supplies.

Policy point 1 (falling domestic prices) reduces the attractiveness of imported goods generally, and particularly of imported goods for which there are acceptable domestic substitutes. Examples of imported products and services of typical low-per-capita-income countries for which the demand is likely to decrease with falling domestic prices are wheat flour, education, foreign travel, refined sugar, shoes, and gasoline. The effect of this development would be to make more foreign exchange available for other purposes and to reduce drastically the pressures for exchange controls which are so detrimental to good relations with foreign investors. In addition, when direct controls over the uses of foreign exchange become necessary to reduce the importation of consumer goods in order to make foreign exchange available to repatriate profits, other political and economic events arise which are harmful to a development program.[29]

In addition, a low-per-capita-income country becomes a more attractive place to reinvest earnings when low taxes on profits are combined with low production costs. The effect of this is to reduce the quantity of profits seeking repatriation. This tendency is accelerated if at the

---

[27] This has been a real problem in the development of efficient industrial production and is an important portion of the strength of the cartel and colonial development of European nations. The European Common Market and other steps toward regionalism and away from strict nationalism are new efforts aimed at elimination of the handicap (C).

[28] See footnote 10.

[29] Again, the argument cannot be developed. It is another position that has been developed by Professor Ragnar Nurske (S) and with which Professor Raymond F. Mikesell agrees (O).

same time government economic leadership is expanding the quantity of social capital and through international agreements is reducing the difficulties encountered by domestic producers in entering foreign markets.[30] These agreements become much easier to negotiate when high import duties are not needed to restrict consumer-type spending or to protect domestic producers from foreign goods produced under lower cost conditions.

The same reasons that would make a low-per-capita-income country, utilizing the policy being tested, a more attractive place to reinvest domestic earnings of both domestic and foreign companies, as was pointed out above, would also cause this country to be more attractive for new private foreign investment. This new foreign investment directly increases the availability of funds to meet repatriation demands, while the encouragement of reinvestment and the reduced general import incentive due to changed price interrelationships reduce the demand for foreign exchange. In addition, as previously mentioned, 1) the demand for foreign exchange is likely to be decreased because of a) the increased incentive for saving money and b) the reduced inventories due to the unprofitability of inventory speculation; and 2) the supply of foreign exchange is likely to be increased because of a) the expansion of exports and b) the expansion of foreign balances kept in domestic currency.

References

A. Buchanan, Norman S., and Ellis, Howard S., *Approaches to Economic Development*. New York: The Twentieth Century Fund, 1955.

B. Burns, A. R., *Comparative Economic Organization*. New York: Prentice-Hall, 1955. P. 696.

C. Chase Manhattan Bank, *The New European Market*, New York, July 1958.

D. Felix, David, "Profit Inflation and Industrial Growth." *The Quarterly Journal of Economics*, August 1956. P. 462.

E. Hagen, Everett E., *Economic Development and Cultural Change*. April 1957. P. 208.

F. Hamilton, E. J., "American Treasure and the Rise of Capitalism."

G. Hansen, Alvin H., *Business Cycles and National Income*. New York: W. W. Norton, 1951.

H. Hicks, Ursula K., *British Public Finances 1880-1952*. London: London University Press, 1954. P. 877.

I. Institute of Inter-American Affairs, Foreign Operations Administration, *The Development of Brazil*. Washington, D. C., 1953. P. 39.

J. Keynes, J. M., *Treatise on Money*. London.

---

[30] Foreign private investment can be hastened by favorable tax treatment of profits and low costs, but the size of foreign investment is perhaps as dependent upon social and primary investment financed by the domestic government. This point is emphasized by Raymond F. Mikesell (P).

K. Lewis, W. Arthur, *The Theory of Economic Growth*. London: George Allen and Unwin, Ltd., 1955. P. 405.

L. Lindholm, Richard W., *et al., Principles of Money and Banking*. New York: W. W. Norton, 1954. P. 59.

M. Mason, Edward S., *Economic Planning in Underdeveloped Areas*. New York: Fordham University Press, 1958. P. 49.

N. Meade, James E., *Planning and the Price Mechanism*. New York: Macmillan, 1949. P. 7.

O. Mikesell, Raymond F., "Economic Doctrines Reflected in U.N. Reports." *American Economic Review*, May 1954. P. 580.

P. Mikesell, Raymond F., *Promoting United States Private Investment Abroad*. Washington, D. C.: National Planning Association, 1957.

Q. Nef, U. U., "Prices and Industrial Capitalism in France and England, 1540-1640." *Essays in Economic History*, edited by E. M. Carus-Wilson. London: Edward Arnold, 1954. Pp. 108-134.

R. *Newsweek*, "What Worries the Overseas Investor Most." 5 November 1956.

S. Nurske, Ragnar, "Some International Aspects of the Problem of Economic Development." *American Economic Review*, May 1952. P. 574.

T. Polanyi, Michael, *The Logic of Liberty*. Chicago: University of Chicago Press, 1951. Pp. 154-155.

U. Simkin, C. G. F., *The Instability of a Dependent Economy*. London: Oxford University Press, 1951. P. 52.

V. Stead, William H., *The Economic Development of Puerto Rico*. Washington, D. C.: National Planning Association, 1958.

W. U.N. ECAFE, *Annual Report*. (Economic and Social Council, Supplement no. 5, p. 24, par. 232) 1955.

X. United Nations, *Processes and Problems of Industrialization in the Underdeveloped Countries*. 1955. Pp. 70-73.

Y. U. S. Department of Commerce, *Factors Limiting U.S. Investment Abroad*, Part II. Washington, D. C., 1954.

Z. Vakil, C. N., and Brahmanand, P. R., *Planning for an Expanding Economy*, Bombay: Vora and Co., 1956. P. 297.

The Farm:
Misused Income Expansion
Base of Emerging Nations

*This selection is taken from the May 1961 issue of the
Journal of Farm Economics published at Michigan State
University in East Lansing.*

*Stated very broadly, Professor Lindholm's thesis is that
agriculture in the underdeveloped countries should be
treated as an industry rather than a way of life, and that
industrializing agriculture should have a high priority
in the developmental efforts of these countries. This belief is opposed to the tendency of both emerging nations
and their advisors from the United States to make minor
changes in agricultural techniques and not to conduct
major overhauls that would make agriculture a surplus-
producing industry.*

For many thousands of years the productivity of labor and the technical procedures used in agriculture remained unchanged. Agriculture
in 1200 A.D. Europe was little different from agriculture in 500 B.C.
Egypt or 1500 A.D. Inca Peru or, for that matter, 1961 Viet-Nam.[1]
Finally, in America and Western Europe of the late 19th century, the
ancient methods of producing food and the institutional organization
began to move step by step toward industrial agriculture as it is known
today in these sections of the world. The productivity of manpower used
in agriculture in the United States[2] caught up with the level in industry largely as a result of the extensive experimental and applied work
carried out under the great stimulation of our colleges of agriculture.

---

[1] Henri Pierenne, *Economic and Social History of Medieval Europe* (London:
Routledge J. Kegan, 1936), pp. 58-86; Sally Falk Moore, *Power and Property in
Inca Peru* (New York: Columbia University Press, 1958), p. 19; and Price
Gittinger, "Agrarian Reform," *Viet-Nam—The First Five Years*, R. W. Lind-
holm, ed. (East Lansing: Michigan State University Press, 1959), pp. 200-212.

[2] Henry Underwood Faulkner, *American Economic History*, 4th ed. (New
York: Harper & Bros., 1938), pp. 447-476.

This very fundamental but largely 20th century aspect of the industrial revolution is of utmost importance to the low-per-capita-income countries of the world. Their failure to emphasize it in development programs is explained by many historical, behavioral, and general political and economic considerations. This paper will briefly point out and analyze these factors while developing an approach for introducing modern industrial agriculture into these economies.

As much as 60 to 70 or even 80 per cent of the people of the emerging nations continue to scratch out a living practicing agriculture as it was practiced in 18th century Europe. These people and their very low productivity form the obvious crux of a development program. The average person of these nations cannot enjoy the minimum requisites of decent food and shelter; nor can he enjoy education, the arts, or a gradual expansion of machine use unless productivity of the major industry is expanded.

Why Agriculture Remained Handicraft

Mr. H. Venkatasubbiah, in an ambitious study, *Indian Economy Since Independence,* fails to include any careful discussion of land use or of the agricultural industry.[3] This neglect cannot, of course, be explained by the unimportance of agriculture as a contributor to the gross national product, by the small number of people engaged in the activity, or by the lack of seriousness of the problems. It can only be explained in terms of Mr. Venkatasubbiah's belief that agriculture is not really an industry but a way of life. If agriculture is a way of life and not an industry, nothing could be more natural than to exclude it when considering strides taken and to be taken in improving the balance of international trade, and to deal with it only when talking of village life and folkways generally.[4]

It seems to be well established in the free world group of emerging nations that modernization of the new evolving societies requires modern steel mills and even wells to provide relatively pure water. It also seems to be accepted that commercial fertilizer plants are required. But the development of a highly productive, surplus-producing agriculture seems not to be necessary.[5]

It is not possible to trace the sources of this position with the exact-

---

[3] H. Venkatasubbiah, *Indian Economy Since Independence* (New York: Institute of Pacific Relations, 1959).

[4] Oscar Lewis, *Village Life in Northern India* (Urbana: University of Illinois Press, 1958), pp. 31-111; and John E. de Young, *Village Life in Modern Thailand* (Berkeley: University of California Press, 1955), pp. 76-146.

[5] For example, this is a good description of the situation in Korea. See *A Report on the University of Oregon Advisory Mission to the Korean Economic Development Council, 1959-1961* (Eugene: University of Oregon, 1961).

ness that one desires. However, some of the elements which seem to go into making it up can be considered within the context of this discussion.

1. The new agricultural experts of these emerging nations have been greatly influenced by American professors of agriculture. Many of these professors have been imbued with the idea of the family farm in the United States. And even though they saw the family farm in India, let us say, to be quite different from its United States counterpart, they still advocated the family farm because it seemed to be the answer to Communist propaganda of land for the landless.[6]

Therefore, the tremendous prestige of American agriculture was thrown aside for some rather vague concept of the good old days memorialized in the ballads of all peoples, when every man was his own boss and lived a fabled life on his acreage.

2. Observers from the evolving countries saw that agriculture remained primitive (nonmechanized) in areas highly developed in manufacturing and transportation; e.g., pre-World War II France and Germany. Thus, it seemed to be normal for a development program to be partial, with the people on the land living and working largely as they had during the past thousand years or so, while goods were transported with the aid of giant diesels and assembly lines typified fabrication. As a result, these observers recommended to their governments that programs along this line were suitable.

3. The large number of persons absorbed in agriculture along traditional lines seems to be a practical barrier to any significant new approach. The question—What would happen to all of the people now on the land if modern American agriculture were introduced?—has been too big or too nebulous a question for planners to face.[7]

The land use policy of the emerging nations in 1961 is the result of the above combination of circumstances, and it has seldom been openly discussed in terms of development goals and production effi-

---

[6] The situation in many of the emerging nations has been similar to that described by Lucy E. Textor as it existed in Czechoslovakia after World War I: "Before the matter (land reform) could be studied from all points of view, the land-hungry people forced the issue. The temper of the time was such that provision for the expropriation of the giant estates had to be made without delay. This must never be forgotten in passing judgment upon the law of April 16, 1919." Lucy E. Textor, *Land Reform in Czechoslovakia* (London: George Allen & Unwin, 1923), p. 140.

[7] For example, "... the Mysore Land Revenue Revision Committee came to the conclusion that all schemes dealing with the evil of subdivision foundered on the rock of inheritance and, therefore, suggested that until there was redistribution of population from agriculture to industry, it would not be opportune to interfere with laws of inheritance." Govindal D. Patel, *The Indian Land Problem and Legislation* (Bombay: N. M. Tripathi, 1954), p. 250.

ciency.[8] Yet the record is abundantly clear that Japan's resurgence in the post-war period was fundamentally related to the reduction of the percentage of the Japanese labor in agriculture from 49.9 per cent in 1947 to 37.9 per cent in 1955.[9] The original downfall of feudalism in Japan was propelled by agriculture; and it is often forgotten that even Puerto Rico's rapid income expansion is agriculturally rooted.[10]

Two fundamental errors run throughout the entire gamut of current agricultural policy in the emerging nations within the United States orbit. First, a failure to establish programs that reflect the depth of the revolt that is taking place among the people of these nations;[11] and second, a failure to fully utilize America's leadership in agriculture.

Typically, technical development programs have established practices to improve conditions somewhat, but largely keep the old procedures and old institutional relationships untouched. Sometimes the programs have obviously been aimed only at countering some move or pledge made by the Communists. Neither of these types of approaches is adequate.[12]

When agriculture is carried out largely as a method by which people earning their subsistence from the land produce their own food and fiber, plus thermal units needed for heating and cooking, the production parameters are very different from those existing under modern conditions.[13] Subsistence agriculture does not fit the requirements for

---

[8] William Bredo skirts the edge of the problem, but his main concern is with decentralization of industry. He does, however, emphasize the importance of mechanized agriculture to economic development and fully recognizes it to be a slow process. William Bredo, "Rural Industrialization for Agricultural Development," *Journal of Farm Economics*, December 1959, pp. 1332-1344.

[9] H. Ouchi, *et al.*, *Nihon Keizai Tokei Shu*—Collections of Japanese Economic Statistics (Tokyo: Nihon Nyoron, 1958).

[10] Reuben E. Slesinger, a bit unrealistically perhaps, states in regard to Puerto Rico, "It typifies the usual course of development: improved agricultural practices, mechanization of agriculture, need for fewer workers on the farms, rising unemployment, migration to the cities, industrialization in the cities, reduced birth rates." "Some Comments on Nonagricultural Possibilities for Raising the Levels of Living of Underdeveloped Nations," *American Economic Review*, May 1956, p. 335.

[11] "They are in revolt not merely against the West, but against their own past . . . " Christopher Dawson, *The Movement of World Revolution* (New York: Sheed & Ward, 1959), p. 103.

[12] That India has been going down the wrong road in agriculture is now widely realized in Indian economic development circles. "The urgent task of the 1960's will be to underpin the Five Year Plans with effective policies of agricultural production and distribution. What has been achieved for such commercial crops as jute shows that it can be done." Geoffrey Tyson, "India Plans for the Sixties," *Lloyds Bank Review*, April 1960, p. 17.

[13] Vernon W. Ruttan, "Research on the Economics of Technological Change in American Agriculture," *Journal of Farm Economics*, November 1960, p. 743.

efficient production of the products utilizing land as a production base.

If it is true that traditional agriculture cannot meet price competition of commercial agriculture and that commercial agriculture does not naturally evolve from traditional peasant agriculture, then a very large portion of our agricultural policy advice and agriculture assistance dispensed to underdeveloped areas has been wrong.[14] It is also true that much of our technical assistance in agriculture which has been aimed at providing small peasant ownership plots and improved techniques for operating these plots will not do the job. The failure to sufficiently emphasize agriculture as a major industry encountering worldwide competitive conditions and going through a technological development of considerable scope must be set down as a major weakness of much economic planning being developed in the emerging nations.[15]

Obviously, what is required is a policy that is revolutionary in the deepest sense, but one that will not destroy the stability which must be maintained if democratic-capitalistic progress is to be made. A program of this sort would permit modern agriculture to be introduced at a date as rapid as the human and technical resources could be developed.

Industrialization Priorities

The basic economic relationship of a program that uses agriculture as the core of a development program can be understood by persons

---

[14] The Food and Agriculture Organization of the United Nations in its *The State of Food and Agriculture, 1958*, in Table 11-6, p. 21, summarizes net exports by volume of *all* agricultural products on the basis of an index with 1951-1953 $=100$. For the Far East (excluding China) the index was 179 in 1955, 55 in 1956, and 17 in 1957. For Latin America the general situation was better; the index average for 1934-1938 was 114, and in 1957 it was 110.

In the same report on page 18 it is reported that "a poor crop in India (1957) coincided with an increased demand, made it necessary to restrict movements of grains, resume procurement, and increase imports. In Pakistan food shortages were reported in some areas." And on page 19, "Exports of agricultural products from Latin America declined . . . "

The basic agricultural industries of the emerging countries have been declining rather than expanding as would be necessary if they were to provide the surpluses required for industrialization.

[15] The general attitude existing in many emerging nations toward the landlord and how he is distinguished from the large owner in industries other than agriculture is well stated in the following selection from the National Planning Board of Pakistan, *Pakistan First Five Year Plan 1955-1960*, December 1957, p. 318.

We consider that the ownership of land is clearly distinguished from other forms of wealth. Landowners who do not manage and cultivate the land themselves, with very few exceptions, do little to increase its productivity. By contrast, the owners of most other forms of wealth are usually progressive and provide increasing employment by their activities.

with only a nodding acquaintance with the science of economics. The relationship is: If more food or as much food can be produced with fewer direct laborers, then more persons can be supported and are thus available to carry forward activities only indirectly related to food production as well as activities completely unrelated to food production.[16] This is the fundamental relationship underlying economic development of most of the emerging nations. Or, to put it somewhat differently, a developed country has a larger portion of its people employed as schoolteachers, technicians, dentists, food packagers, assembly line workers, and concert pianists, because a smaller portion of the people is needed to raise the food required to meet consumption needs.[17]

With this basic proposition stated, the first job of economic planning for development seems obvious. It is 1) to maintain and increase agricultural production while reducing the number of persons engaged in agriculture, and 2) to develop ways to use the persons no longer required directly in food production.

Planners have typically backed into this fundamental aspect of increasing per capita productivity. They back in by first making provision for the establishment of certain industries that are to provide employment outside of agriculture. The first attack is made in this backward direction because the goods these industries would produce are not being produced in quantity in the country and because there seems to be an abundance of unemployed and partially unemployed persons to man the new firms. Also, it is easier politically to develop manufacturing industries first because this has become the accepted folklore of the way economic development takes place.[18]

The implementation of this procedure has certainly been only a partial success. A major shortcoming in both Communist and non-Communist areas has been that the agricultural sector has not been able to provide the food surpluses required to meet the needs of the expanded urban industrial and technical population.[19]

---

[16] Family budget studies show that as much as 80 per cent of income is used to purchase food. Even in the high-income groups in a country as developed as Russia, the family food budget comprises about "43 per cent" of net income left after taxes. David Granick, *The Red Executive* (New York: Doubleday & Co., 1960), p. 116.

[17] "So low is the productivity of Latin American farm workers . . . that it takes three and a half persons working on farms to produce what is contributed to the national wealth by one person engaged in other activities." U. N. Commission for Latin America, *New York Times*, 19 May 1959. Trained observers of the Asian scene have frequently estimated that the marginal productivity of agricultural workers is near zero.

[18] P. T. Bauer, *United States Aid and Indian Economic Development* (Washington, D.C.: American Enterprise Association, 1959), pp. 24-56.

[19] "The Conference considered that careful studies were needed in the whole field of productivity and on agrarian reform in relation to productivity . . . Par-

This shortcoming, although important, is not by any means the only problem which has arisen to plague this approach. Other difficulties in non-Communist areas have included 1) finding markets for goods produced, 2) locating technical and managerial skills required, 3) preventing debasement of the currency, and 4) avoiding rural-urban conflict. These difficulties are sufficiently serious to justify a careful search for another approach.

If, instead of starting with urban industrial growth, one started with rural modernization, the development plan would be based on a much different land-use program and would have a very different overall impact. The typical procedure being followed today in the emerging nations largely considers agricultural land use as on the fringe of the new developments. The procedure considered below follows the simple logic that agriculture is the principal industry of the emerging nations, and it is an industry where labor productivity using modern techniques has expanded very much. Therefore, agriculture is the prime area to be attacked in raising productivity.

A Development Program

Japan's economic development experience must be carefully considered when economic programs are being recommended for today's emerging nations.[20] Japan definitely used agriculture as the keystone of its program.[21] The way agriculture was used was determined by the technology available seventy or ninety years ago and by the cultural, economic, and political conditions of that period.[22]

Current government planning to accelerate development through treating agriculture as an industry and using its expanded per capita

---

ticular emphasis was laid upon the importance of comparative studies on the methods of consolidation of fragmented holdings." Food and Agriculture Organization of the United Nations, *Report of the Ninth Session of the Conference* (Rome, 1958), p. 42.

[20] The arguments of this paper badly need support, for such great academic names in economic development literature as Galbraith, Rostow, and Schultz have argued otherwise. J. K. Galbraith, "Conditions for Economic Change in Underdeveloped Countries," *Journal of Farm Economics,* November 1951, pp. 689-696; W. W. Rostow, "The Take-Off into Self-Sustained Economic Growth," *The Economic Journal,* March 1956, pp. 25-48; and Theodore Schultz, *The Economic Organization of Agriculture* (New York: McGraw-Hill, 1953), pp. 146-151.

Professor Douglas C. North, "Agriculture in Regional Economic Growth," *Journal of Farm Economics,* December 1959, pp. 943-951, forcefully supports a position akin to the one I have developed.

[21] This is brought out repeatedly by Thomas C. Smith in his *The Agrarian Origins of Modern Japan* (Stanford: Stanford University Press, 1959).

[22] "Changes in farming had created 'a surplus'; but the traditional features of agrarian society made it possible for the government to continue to take the surplus over many generations." *Ibid.,* p. 211.

production to support people engaged in a variety of activities might follow a plan along the following lines:

1. The government would provide arrangements for a crash program aimed at educating those who wish to learn modern agricultural methods. This would include instruction on how to operate and repair agricultural machinery. This program would be open to everyone, but the standards of accomplishment that would permit a participant to continue the program should be very high. Students would be paid a substantial salary while carrying on the program.[23]

2. A program would be initiated to buy up land areas and form farms of a size sufficient for sound commercial agriculture. These farms would be sold to the graduates of the above program, and the land purchased would be no greater than the amount needed to meet this requirement. The sale contract would provide for annual payments. Machinery would be financed through rental arrangements worked out with the farm machinery companies. Originally, this activity would be limited to a particular region.

3. The taxes levied on land included in these commercial farms would be based on capitalized value of the farm if modern commercial farming procedures were used. The assessed value of all other agricultural land would be gradually increased to this level.

It is quite possible that higher land taxes will cause the ordinary renter and landowner to increase the efficiency of their operations so that they might enjoy the same income after the higher taxation as they had enjoyed before.[24] If the imposition of land taxes will create pressures leading to a more rapid abandonment of traditional prac-

---

[23] Mr. Patel, in the preface to his book, *The Indian Land Problem and Legislation, op. cit.*, writes: "In the present context of our underdeveloped economy, what is most important is not so much who owns land as how land is cultivated . . . It is no use entrusting cultivation of land to individuals who have neither the ability nor the experience to undertake it." Mr. Patel's solution is cooperative farming.

[24] Sir Stamford Raffles in 1813, when recommending a land reform system providing for the payment of cash rents by the cultivators of Java, said that his land reform would produce "industry, knowledge, and happiness." John Bastin, *Raffles' Ideas on the Land Rent System in Java* (S. Gravenhage-Martinus Nijhoff, 1954), p. 155.

Bauer and Yamey write, "Moreover, the cumpulsory reduction of rents may even reduce output, especially in the short run; this would occur if tenants prefer to take out the windfall gain partly or wholly in the form of more leisure." Peter T. Bauer and Basil S. Yamey, *The Economics of Underdeveloped Countries* (Chicago: University of Chicago Press, 1957), p. 212.

Raffles was talking about the substitution of a free labor and market system for a slave-feudal system. Bauer and Yamey are analyzing the impact of reducing property rights through reduction of rents. Both are also providing support for higher land value taxation as an inducement to greater agricultural productivity.

tices and adoption of more productive practices, it becomes desirable policy on this count alone. If, in addition, the collection of the taxes provides finances to make possible useful collective action, the increase of land taxes is doubly attractive.[25]

High taxes based on the productivity capabilities of modern agricultural land-utilizing techniques is a feasible program and is in many ways the tax most compatible with the conditions encountered in emerging nations.[26] Closely correlating these tax collections with expenditure programs aimed at improving the productivity of the peasants no longer in agriculture should provide a political base capable of effectively combating pressures for the hopeless programs of land reform and family plots.

Agriculture was basic to Japanese development because the government was able to collect substantial agricultural property taxes.[27] In Turkey the government has generally followed a program of industrial agriculture, and the results of mechanization in expanded production have been substantial.[28] The impact, however, has been considerably blunted by the government's inability to collect agricultural taxes.[29]

The impact on labor productivity arising directly from the use of modern techniques and the reduction of the quantity of agricultural labor can be estimated by using some Japanese data. In 1951 the marginal productivity of labor in agriculture in Japan was $217 and in the United States, $2,691. The marginal productivity of one *hectare* (2.471 acres) of land in Japan in 1951 was $193 and in the United States, $28. Despite this high productivity of land and a hard-working farm population, the agricultural industry of Japan in 1951 made less effective use of its factors of production than the agricultural industry of the United States. About 25 per cent of the total difference in real output of agriculture in Japan and the United States is accounted for by "greater land availability in the United States" and about 75 per cent

---

[25] Neo-classical writers had this difference in use of tax-collected funds in mind when they talked of the distinction "between onerous and beneficial rates, the latter being those which were spent in providing services from which ratepayers benefited." Ralph Turvey, *The Economics of Real Property* (London: George Allen & Unwin, 1957), p. 67.

[26] This seems to be the general conclusion of Haskell P. Wald in *Taxation of Agricultural Land in Underdeveloped Economies* (Cambridge: Harvard University Press, 1959).

[27] The land tax of Japan from 1868 to 1881 accounted for 78 per cent of ordinary revenues. These revenues provided the bulk of the savings which the government funneled into investment used to carry forward an industrial program. Thomas C. Smith, *op. cit.*, p. 211.

[28] William H. Nicholls, "Investment in Agriculture in Underdeveloped Countries," *American Economic Review*, May 1955, p. 64.

[29] *Ibid.*, p. 66.

by such influences as "advantages of capital, technology scale, and so on."[30]

4. Persons relieved from performing agricultural activities because their land has been purchased by the government to be sold to the graduates of the agricultural specialists school would be placed on government payrolls if they so desired.[31] These payrolls would be largely met from the added tax receipts arising from the land now operated on a business basis.[32] The government would use these new employees to construct farm-to-city roads, sewers, and other projects and would provide them with evening adult technical training courses and day liberal and technical courses for the children. The increased productivity originating in better land use would spread through the society as the benefits of a generally more efficient use of manpower made itself felt.[33]

5. In the industrial sector, priority would be given to the development of plants producing farm machinery. In the distribution and marketing sectors, priority would be given to those aspects most directly related to agriculture; i.e., agri-business type development.[34]

Emphasis would have to be placed on growing certain agricultural products possessing a favorable international market. Careful planning here can produce "luck" such as Japan enjoyed during her early development period. Raw silk was an agricultural product suited to natural and other conditions existing in Japan, and was also a product that could be sold to earn the foreign exchange needed to finance pur-

---

[30] Toyoki Okabayashi, *Measuring the Contributions of Natural Resources to the National Outputs of the United States and Japan* (University of Oregon, unpublished Ph.D. thesis, 1960), p. 100.

[31] A program to carry on agriculture as a modern industry would go far toward the general upgrading of agriculture as a work career. A recent Philippines study shows " . . . that only 4 per cent mentioned farming as their occupation preference for their children—although the Philippines is primarily an agricultural country." Edward Tiryakian, "Occupational Satisfaction and Aspirations in an Underdeveloped Country: The Philippines," *Economic Development and Cultural Change*, July 1959, p. 437.

[32] "We [the United States] have been producing in recent years on 20 to 25 million acres about the same amount of cotton as we were producing on more than 40 million acres in the period around 1930." Murray R. Benedict, *Can We Solve the Farm Problem?* (New York: The Twentieth Century Fund, 1955), p. 52.

[33] New technical developments are rapidly changing agriculture in Japan. "The Japanese government is drawing up legislation to encourage groupings of farmers into 'corporations', which would purchase tractors and other machines that could be used by all members in turn. About 300 such corporations have already been formed." *New York Times*, 3 January 1960, p. 3.

[34] John H. Davis and Ray A. Goldberg, *A Concept of Agri-Business* (Boston: Harvard Graduate School of Business Administration, 1957).

chase of machines from foreign countries.[35] These exports, added to agricultural tax collections, provided the industrial investment base and support for all the ancillary activities fundamental to Japan's industrial society.

This is a development plan moving gradually from the country to the city. The basic aim of the program is to make better use of manpower and to treat agricultural land as an industrial resource. As the manpower becomes trained and released from agriculture, it will be available to teach in the schools and to play in the orchestras; in other words, the people will enjoy the benefits of economic development.

Conclusion

The basic assumptions of the industrial agriculture development program outlined here are:

1. **More food can be produced by the use of modern agricultural methods with only a fraction of the current manpower located on the farms.**
2. **People living off the farms and carrying out other pursuits do not require any greater quantities of food to meet their requirements than do people on the farms.**
3. **Therefore, if fewer people are needed in agriculture, more people can be fed while carrying on nonagricultural and agriculture-related activities.**

The logic of emphasizing the development of the agricultural industry as the first major step or perhaps the basic platform for an economic development revolution has always seemed by nonprofessional observers to be the correct procedure; but, for reasons mentioned above, it has not been followed.

The alternative to a development program based on industrial agriculture is one based on industrialization of fabrication. The industrialization of fabrication before the industrial agriculture base is developed looks a great deal like building the roof of a building before the foundation and the sidewalls have been completed. Here the foundation is comparable to efficient food production, which provides such a large portion of the immediate consumption requirements of the subsistence societies under consideration. The sidewalls are comparable to all the social and educational adjustments and understandings required of a population when it moves into the modern age.

It is possible to build the roof first, but if this is done, a great deal of effort must be expended to brace and support the roof while the foundation and the sidewalls are under construction.

---

[35] The European production of silk was seriously reduced owing to the outbreak of the pebrine plague, while the demand for silk continued high. D. T. Lakdawala, *International Aspects of Indian Economic Development* (London: Oxford University Press, 1951), p. 11, quoted in Albert O. Hirshman, *The Strategy of Economic Development* (New Haven: Yale University Press, 1958), p. 172.

Environment Adjustment Related to Economic Development

The following selection was originally given as a lecture by Professor Lindholm at a 1953 symposium at Peshawar, Pakistan, sponsored by the Fulbright group in that country. The lecture was given in its present form at the National Institute of Administration in Saigon in 1956, and appeared that year in a mimeographed book prepared by the Michigan State economic advisors in South Viet-Nam.

This lecture makes clear the problems involved in the transition from a feudal agrarian to a capitalistic society in which agriculture is an industry rather than a way of life.

All the large societies of the world, when they developed beyond tribal organization, utilized an economic arrangement which is called feudal. It seems that primitive subsistence agriculture, with production relying nearly entirely on human and animal power, always organized itself around a dominant landowner group who lived off the produce of workers tied to the soil. In turn the minor landlords owed services in kind to the larger landlords, with the ruler being the largest and most powerful landlord. This organization and its tendency to stagnation and reduction of initiative and commerce has varied little from nation to nation. The existing organization of production of much of Pakistan, for example, is very similar to that which existed in France under the Bourbons and England under the Tudors. It is into this rather unfriendly environment that the machine has been introduced, and it is this set of relationships that the machine disrupts.

This similarity of organization of production in thickly populated areas, despite great cultural differences, seems to indicate that the mode of production has determined the organization of society. Therefore, the change of the method of production by the introduction of the machine is very likely to require a basic change of the principles of the organization. This discussion assumes that the development in countries introducing machine production techniques today will be roughly similar to the development in countries that have already passed through this stage.

The generality of feudal organization, plus the acceptance of the idea that the organization of society is determined by the method of production, permits a description of the environmental problems of the introduction of the machine that is applicable to all underdeveloped countries. Obviously there are minor differences between the feudal society of Peru and that of Pakistan, but these differences do not necessitate a particularized discussion at this point. Also, the exact details of a society that has accepted the machine will vary, such as the difference between pre-war Germany and the United States. Again, these differences need not concern us, for the variations are relatively insignificant.

The feudal society possesses one other ingredient in addition to land ownership and operation and handicraft production that is vital to its healthy functioning. This is a religious sanction and protection of the rights and privileges of the different ranks of the social structure. In all cases this religious sanction has arisen from overemphasizing the portion of the faith of the nation sanctioning privilege and underemphasizing the writings stressing equality.

The first severe impact of the machine in meeting the feudal environment is the creation of unemployment among the workers. One machine attended by five or six partially skilled workers will produce a product that had formerly required the skilled services of hundreds. Also the machine-made product can either be sold at a price so low that the handicraft worker cannot compete or be a superior product that replaces the handicraft article. The machine production of cotton cloth and yarn is an example of the machine replacement of handicraft production through lower cost. The modern sewage system is an example of the provision of a function that replaces another provided under handicraft procedures.

The elimination of the need for hundreds and thousands of workers poses a serious welfare and humanitarian problem. The problem of feeding, housing, and clothing the unemployed is likely to be inadequately managed. The more serious problem of morale and rehabilitation is not likely to be touched.

The creation of unemployment among agricultural workers by the use of machine sowing, cultivation, and harvesting adds to the total unemployed. In the case of agricultural workers, the machine requires the elimination of the feudal relationship between the worker and the landowner. The landowner no longer needs the labor of the occupants of his land, but these occupants have written and unwritten sanction to remain. The landowner faces the serious problem of how to rid the land of the now useless inhabitants. The inhabitants in turn clamor to be given plots of land for their own cultivation in the ancient methods.

The demand for the breaking up of the feudal estates into small, personally owned plots is a procedure to prevent the machine from causing unemployment on the land and basically to prevent a reduction of the agricultural population. Handicraft nonagricultural workers also fight to retain their ancient relationships. The government is pressured to subsidize handicraft production and roadblocks are placed in the way of technical improvements.

The unemployment of nonagricultural workers through the introduction of machines is less today than formerly. Today the use of machines in an underdeveloped country frequently causes a reduction of imports and has a tendency to cause unemployment abroad rather than domestically. Therefore, the agricultural unemployment arising from the machine and the reorganization it necessitates have become much greater problems than the unemployment of handicraft nonagricultural workers. However, the problem of unemployment of nonagricultural workers continues to be a difficult adjustment that must be made in introducing the machine culture.

A second early adjustment is the transfer and acquisition of economic power by the owners of machines. The power of machine owners is resisted because they are considered to be intruders and to cause a dilution of the economic power formerly held exclusively by traders and landowners. Traders, for example, fight the tariff protection needed by infant industries. They are given at least tacit support by the landowners who prefer cheap imported goods to slightly inferior and perhaps higher-priced domestic goods.

If the owner of these new machines is the government rather than individuals, this additional economic power rests in the government. Because the government will be dominated by the landowners and to some extent by the merchant groups, the introduction of the machine under these circumstances does not cause a dilution of economic power. This is the adjustment to the new environment that is easiest. It fits neatly into the social and economic arrangement existing in underdeveloped countries. Whether the adjustment is one which will utilize the machine most efficiently is quite another question. Also, there is the problem of the landowners and merchants being unable to continue to control the government as the managers of the machines increase their power with the growth of the economic importance of machine production.

The feudal social arrangement provides only a limited place for propertyless citizens working with hand and brain. There are a few opportunities as managers of estates, servants of the ruler, army officers, merchants, and teachers. And that is about all. Most of these positions are directly dependent upon the good favor of the ruler. The introduction of the machine requires a considerable change. Large numbers of highly trained people are required to service the machines and manage the operations of machines. In addition, the necessity of general literacy changes the character of the laboring population and greatly increases the importance of educators.

The effect of these changes is the establishment of other groups within the society that possess the necessary economic independence and education to challenge the dominant position of the feudal groups. Again, the solution of having these groups dependent upon the government presents itself as an attractive solution to the old feudal dominant groups. The ability of the old groups to continue to dominate the government depends on their ability to prevent the new groups from gaining power. To a considerable degree this amounts to convincing the new groups that it is in their interest to accept the goals of the old groups. An aspect of this regrouping is likely to be a separation of management from labor. Management (government or private) accepts the attitude of the feudal ruling groups and labor is relegated to a position analogous to that of the serfs.

The relegation of laborers working with machines to the inferior position of laborers in a handicraft-feudal economy is at the best an unstable situation. An additional adjustment will become necessary when management finds its profits can be increased by working the laborers shorter hours and by paying higher wages to attract the most intelligent and to stimulate improvement of skills. As the laborers acquire literacy, a necessary skill for a laborer working with machines, they became aware of the wage potential of their position. In addition, the literacy of laborers under conditions of something less than a complete censorship will create conditions (under either government or private ownership) leading to an independent political movement of workers. The effect of these developments will lead to new adjustments. The violence involved and the difficulty encountered in developing the new relationships will be in direct proportion to the degree in which the machine owners and managers tie their interests to those of the old feudal leaders. We see this violence erupting today in Hungary and Poland, and we have observed it in the past in England and the United States.

The final major adjustment is in how the productivity of the machine is to be divided. It is perhaps the most difficult and incomplete adjustment because it is always being changed to meet new power relations. The previous discussion has made it quite evident that the machine encountering a well-organized feudal society causes serious disruptions of the power centers. Basically the machine is a revolutionary force. The most fundamental aspect of a revolution is the change it causes in the relative economic well-being of the different sections of the society. This is also true of the machine-caused revolution, but in addition the machine creates a large additional product that must be divided in some fashion.

Again the rules of the feudal society are at hand. These rules basically assume that income from productive activity is divided into two parts—rents to the owners of resources and subsistence to laborers. When applied to machine production it provides an inadequate stimulus to efficiency. In addition, it is likely to be quite unsatisfactory to the three major elements of machine production—the laborers, the managers, and the organizers or entrepreneurs. The production of a machine society is most conveniently divided into rent, interest, profits, and wages.

Under conditions of abundant investment funds the portion going to rent is likely to be very small, for an indefinite number of equally efficient plants may be constructed until the demand is completely satisfied. In the feudal economy, with land the basic element of production, large rents arise because of the very limited quantity of first-class agricultural land.

In a machine economy the provider of funds is frequently protected from income fluctuations and his return is paid as interest. In a feudal economy interest as an income is likely to arise only under emergency conditions and is frequently associated with disaster. Because of this, interest payments are frequently prohibited or are considered an undesirable type of income. The provider of funds in a feudal society is the landlord. Actually, under the feudal production conditions, the need for funds to finance operations is very limited. In a machine economy very large quantities of investment funds are needed, and the tapping of a very important source of these funds requires an assurance that annual amounts will be paid for their use in monetary units with a purchasing power approximately equal to those loaned. This type of payment is called interest.

Introduction and Use
of the Machine

Like the preceding lecture, the following selection was also given in Pakistan in 1953 and later in Saigon in 1956.

Here Professor Lindholm does not attempt to establish a general program suitable for economic development, but rather explains the problems of social change that arise under any such program.

Perhaps the first machine man uses is made of levers and pullies that increase the weight he can move or lift. The next step in the use of the machine is to harness power other than human. This additional power is supplied by animals—oxen, camels, horses—and then by the direct application of flowing water to a water wheel. Later, with the development of technology, the power is usually supplied by the steam engine and the electric dynamo.

The machine, in addition to providing the possibility of moving or raising additional weight without requiring the services of more men, makes possible the production of goods at a lower cost and the production of new types of goods. The reduced cost arises from the greater efficiency with which inanimate energy can be applied and from the lower cost of providing a given quantity of inanimate energy. The new products arise from the greater precision and the greater concentration of energy than are possible with handicraft procedures.

The manner in which the machine is introduced can affect the possibility of a more comfortable life. For example, the restriction of the machine process to areas where all or nearly all of the production is exported will not directly create a more comfortable life for the inhabitants of these areas. In addition, if the new machinery is closely held and laborers are paid a minimum wage, only a small number of people possess additional purchasing power as the result of the introduction of the machine. The fortunate benefactors are likely to use up a considerable portion of their earnings attempting to ape the habits of the so-called elite of the old machine economies and of feudal society. Under these conditions the effect of the increased productivity of the machine is little more than the creation of several wealthy families living in modern feudal splendor amidst unabated poverty.

The introduction of the machine to produce products largely for the export market with the ownership of the processes vested in the hands of wealthy individuals or families has many inherent weaknesses, but it has happened frequently enough to warrant consideration. The development of oil and mineral resources are excellent examples of the procedure, such as the exploitation of the tin resources of Bolivia and the oil resources of Kuwait.

The control over the reproductivity of the machine, the products of which are sold abroad, can be made much more acceptable if the income is used to develop other domestic industries. This program requires that profits of the industry be invested domestically to increase the productivity of domestic workers. To carry forward this program, profits must not be spent on luxury goods but rather must be saved. The savings must not be hoarded in gold or silver or invested in land, foreign securities, or enterprises, but must be used to finance domestic enterprises utilizing modern production procedures.

It is the realization of the desirability of local investment that has caused nations to restrict the withdrawal of profits made by foreign firms. The general restrictions on the importation of luxury goods and encouragement of the importation of productive machinery is legislative action in the same direction. The difficulty with this legislation is that reducing incentives through restricting the uses to which profits may be placed could have a greater restrictive than expansive effect on productive investment. Also, legislation of this sort is apt to have its greatest impact on industries selling domestically. The domestic seller must always make provision through official channels for foreign exchange, and therefore legislation restricting withdrawal of profits can always be strictly enforced. On the other hand, firms selling abroad, which are not directly increasing the domestic standard of living, can readily avoid the restrictions by misrepresenting their receipts.

None of the nations seeking to expand investment have instituted a program restricting domestic luxury expenditures or investments in land (except through restriction of the size of holdings of certain types of land). It is rather doubtful if legislation directly restricting these expenditures is enforceable. The best that could be expected would be a tax and monetary program discouraging investment in land and an attitude toward life rather similar to that of the reformation period in Europe. However, the action would be aimed at all owners of highly productive facilities and not exclusively at owners of productive facilities closely held who sell their products abroad.

Another aspect of investment in productive facilities, the products of which are sold abroad, is that they alone provide the foreign exchange required to purchase modern equipment. For example, most of the ability of Bolivia and Kuwait to purchase goods produced in the United States arises from the sale abroad of tin and oil. The industries producing goods for domestic consumption do not directly provide any foreign purchasing power. In fact, the original investment in machines and a continuing expenditure for parts and maybe raw materials must be financed with exchange arising from other sources. This relationship between the productivity of the machine producing for foreign sale and the machine producing for domestic use has caused many economic ministers to favor the machine producing for sale abroad. It is sometimes forgotten that this comparison may be misleading, for all of the foreign exchange arising from selling products of the machine meeting the requirements of a foreign market may be used to purchase abroad products that could have been provided by a machine producing for domestic use.

In comparing machines producing for the foreign and the domestic market, the real economic effect can be quite different from that which is apparent through examination of export data. For this reason the analysis of the desirability of the machine must go deeper than a mere consideration of direct results. The best guide to be used is not whether the machine provides foreign exchange or meets domestic needs but rather the extent to which it increases the productivity of workers. The use of this test eliminates the apparent greater desirability that has on occasion been bestowed upon machines producing goods wanted by certain groups. Instead the test is placed where it belongs—on productivity. Fortunately, this basis can be utilized without placing into operation elaborate schemes of control.

Basically the economic productivity is judged by the increase of the monetary value of the product, less the allocated portion of the cost of the machine, that can be produced by a given number of workers utilizing the machine. If two workers in one year without the machine can produce a product valued at 100 monetary units and with the machine a product valued at 150 monetary units, and the additional cost arising from the use of the machine is 25 monetary units, the machine has increased productivity by 25 monetary units. This machine would be installed and utilized, prior to one requiring equal investment but with an increased productivity of only 15 units, by a businessman operating within a free economy. In other words, the market can be relied upon to make the correct investment decisions. Complicated regulations and control are unnecessary. The existence of this relationship is very important to underdeveloped countries, for they can not afford to engage in all the expensive regulative devices that would be required to ration investment on the basis of provision or utilization of foreign exchange.

This simplified approach to the determination of machine priority is criticized in a number of ways. Before going into these criticisms, let it be realized at the outset that in individual instances a more perfect device could be utilized. However, underdeveloped countries have a great shortage of technicians, and therefore any regulative program will fall far short of its aim. And the technicians used to regulate cannot be used to produce. These are two fundamental and important aspects of underdevelopment; i.e., shortage of technicians and shortage of production.

A criticism frequently given is that the test of productivity provided by value on the market is unacceptable because the basis instead should be on welfare. Therefore the machine should first be used to produce for the very poor. The point is well taken, but its implementation would require tax collections from the rich or some other source of financing and also require partial abandonment of the efficiency of the market in allocating production. This judgment of productivity would fail to provide the stimulus to middle-class initiative, which is vital to the development of underdeveloped nations. The problems inherent in the use of this basis are many, and its ability to do any more than to maintain a slightly larger population at subsistence is to be doubted.

The desirability of a judgment based on the effectiveness in providing foreign exchange has already been considered and need not be reiterated. It is, however, one very vociferous source of criticism of the simple market test of productivity. Rather than encourage relatively unproductive industries with an export market, it would be desirable to understand the indirect effects of this action and the possible desirability of inaugurating a policy that proves more attractive to foreign investors.

A plan of economic development such as a four-year plan is another device recommended as an improvement over the market's judgment. Here again many technicians will be needed to administer and enforce regulations if the plan is other than that which profitability in the market would establish. Why have a plan if the plan is merely an outline of the development that the market would set if left alone?

The idea of a plan of development received its impetus in Russia after that country had decided to carry on all production and distribution through government facilities. The government has operated on the basis of a dogma that had been extracted by the ruling class from the writings of Marx. The result of this decision was that a free market was no longer available and therefore recourse to a detailed plan of development was necessary. If a nation has not made a similar decision, the utilization of a detailed plan is superfluous. The planning required of a nation operating under liberal principles is limited largely to the provision of social capital.

Planning the entire economy of the nation over a number of years inherently possesses a number of weaknesses that should not be lightly assumed. First, of course, is the inability to forecast economic possibilities for four or seven years in advance. The result of such an effort could be the creation of many new and avoidable difficulties. If the economy is forced into a plan that because of changed circumstances no longer fits, a considerable waste of resources is certain. Secondly, some portions of the program will go forward quickly and efficiently and other portions will become bogged down. This becomes a basic problem and involves the decision whether to complete the portion that is proceeding satisfactorily and then leave it idle while the bogged-down facility is completed, or to wastefully attempt to transfer labor and capital from the efficient area, leaving it incomplete, in an attempt to speed up the inefficient area.

If under a planned program two or more groups are permitted to have varied political, social, and economic ideas, a change of government leaders who have a different basis of judgment and list of priorities is quite possible. The result is that when one plan is only partially complete its scope and form is changed. The effect, of course, is likely to be waste and confusion. This difficulty again shows the suitability of a detailed economic plan to a country where no differences of opinion are permitted and its unsuitability to countries organized on another basis.

The third type of income vital to a machine economy is profit. The role of profit, in fact the very concept of profit, is largely unknown to the feudal economy. The portion of the productivity of the machine economy paid as profit varies considerably from year to year and from industry to industry. The function of profit in directing the quantity of investment to be made in a particular industry is performed through this variation. High profits in a particular industry act to increase investment in that area and low profits within an industry act to decrease investment. Profits also provide a constant stimulus to efficient operation and to the introduction of the most efficient production techniques. Annual variation of average profit levels provides a guide to monetary and fiscal policy actions.

Rent continues to exist in the machine economy but its importance is considerably reduced. This is partially so because the portion of national income arising directly from the use of the scarce land resource is less. An additional reason is the much greater volatility of the machine economy than that of the feudal economy. This volatility causes a constant shifting of relationships, and therefore income from scarcity takes on more of the characteristics of profit or return from management than that of rent. Rent in a machine economy becomes of increased importance if, because of monopoly or excess regulation, the inherent characteristics of the continuous process of adoption and casting aside are abandoned. Actually the machine economy loses a basic portion of its unique forces working towards progress if either monopoly or very close government regulation arises.

The payment of wages in a feudal economy is to cover subsistence costs. In a machine economy wages are paid at a level to approximate the contribution of labor to production. The contribution is best measured by deducting from national income the cost of the machine and managerial costs plus profits adequate to perform the functions allocated to profits. The size of national income is set by all the conditions of the market, which are, of course, too varied to be analyzed at this time. Wages of a machine economy take between 70 and 80 per cent of national income, and they in turn as purchasing power are the source of about the same portion of total expenditures. If the portion of national income paid to wages falls, laborers are discontent due to high profits, rents, and interest receipts. In addition, expenditures are very likely to fall below the level required to clear the markets. This concept of wages necessary for an effective machine economy is quite contrary to wages in a feudal economy and can be the source of considerable conflict before the adjustment is made.

Public Finance
and Economic Development

This selection is taken from "A Report on the University of Oregon Advisory Mission to the Korean Economic Council, 1959-1961," published by the University of Oregon Press in Eugene.

A most interesting suggestion here is Professor Lindholm's proposal of an international fiscal agency.

I wish to outline briefly the evolution of thinking in the area of fiscal policy and expansion of investment rate in low-per-capita-income countries. Next I shall briefly summarize where I think we are at the present time relative to fiscal policy and economic development. Finally, I wish to push back just a bit the frontiers of thinking in this area.

After World War II, when the need for rapid expansion of income in low-per-capita-income nations began to force itself upon the thinking of the world's economists and leaders, recourse was made to an answer that lies in Keynesian economics. The answer seemed to be : Use government deficit financing through the new central banks. This could be used safely as long as unemployed labor existed—and certainly low-per-capita-income countries had an abundance of unemployed labor. Therefore, the program could be actively pushed for quite some time.

It was soon learned that the relationships which had made Keynesian-type deficit spending somewhat appropriate under unemployment conditions in Western Europe and the United States in the 1930's did not exist in the low-per-capita-income countries. Deficit financing of this type did not bring about economic development and it did not bring jobs to the unemployed. It did, however, disorganize the economy with raging inflation and forced weak governments to allocate much too great a portion of these resources to control activities—from rationing of consumer necessities to preventing capital flights.

The next popular theory continued the idea of government-directed investment but provided that the funds were to come from tax revenues in excess of expenditures rather than from central bank credit. This concept gained renown in centers of learning and in government economic planning circles.

A few years of experience have made everyone realize what most finance ministers had been saying all along: It would not be possible to administer a tax load in excess of the level required to carry out normal government functions. Actually, the finance ministers have found it very difficult to raise sufficient revenues to cover normal government operations. The exceptions to this generalization are the nations receiving large oil royalties. However, even these countries have not been particularly successful in efforts to get expanded production under way.

In some instances where it became obvious that normal tax revenues would not meet investment needs as well as normal needs and where central bank credit had been ruled out, procedures were initiated to milk revenues from government monopolies and enterprises. In most instances this resulted in loss of working capital by the enterprise or failure of the enterprise to set aside funds to keep its equipment modern and in repair. If prices were raised sufficiently to provide a margin adequate to meet all demands, strict controls of imports became necessary; and a base for high cost, and therefore internationally noncompetitive economy, was developed.

All of these procedures were based upon the idea that the government should provide investment funds. None of the programs, however, relied on attracting voluntary savings as a major source of funds. In all cases the savings to be used to finance investment were to be forced in one way or another. The reasons for this choice are obvious and can be summarized in the statement: Significant quantities of government bonds could not be sold.

Public finance as a tool of expanding economic development has been entering a new and much more sophisticated phase during the past several years. Basically this new phase abandons the concept of government providing funds for investment. The government does not provide significant economic development funds from credit creation, from current revenue, or from public borrowings. Instead, the tax system is developed to encourage reinvestment of earnings and increasing earnings in the hands of those most likely to invest.

This type of fiscal policy provides for low taxation of income reinvested, taxation to encourage retention of profits in the business, low taxation of new domestic and foreign investment, high taxation of consumer and luxury spending, and generally, taxation that encourages resource use and initiative. The new fiscal policy is aimed at taking government fiscal demands off the backs of production and distribution managers who have shown an ability to operate an economic enterprise and who are willing to reinvest earnings in domestic productive activities. It is clear that this type of fiscal policy has made a clean break-away from the first theories and their emphasis on government performing the investment function.

The questions here are:

Will this new type of fiscal policy do what it is supposed to do?

The answer I believe must be a qualified *"yes."* The impact of the fiscal policy will be *most effective* in the case of rather large industrial operations and in agriculture and *least effective* where natural resources are not important in the production base and where the enterprise is a rather informal, family-dominated operation. This is one part of the qualification; another part of the qualification is related to policies and justice in taxation. A tax system based on this concept of economic development is likely to rest more heavily on low income receivers than the tax system it replaces or the tax system existing in high-per-capita-income countries. This will create political difficulties and provide opportunities for demagogues to cause considerable trouble.

Does it go as far as fiscal policy can go in encouraging expanding per capita incomes in low-per-capita-income countries?

The answer I believe must be a qualified *"no."* I say this because I believe that governments must play a more active role than the type of fiscal policy outlined above permits or provides. In considering this point, I shall make an effort to push forward a little bit the frontiers of our thinking relative to fiscal policy and economic development.

The role of the government in economic development cannot be financed by excess tax receipts or central bank credit. This is accepted today. It is doubtful if conditions are going to change sufficiently to make government investment activities in these old ways possible. However, it might be possible that government investment activity could be financed in areas such as power, education, and transportation through borrowing from savers. I believe it is an area of fiscal policy that will be expanding, and that its expansion will fit in very well with the fiscal policy encouraging private investment and expansion of private productive facilities.

There are a number of programs which have been discussed and which could lay the basis for expanded government borrowing from savers. One that has proven useful is the issuance of purchasing power loans and also the development of banking legislation to permit purchasing power savings accounts. It is a practical way to encourage saving and purchase of debt securities in countries where inflation cannot be brought under control.

It is quite possible that in some countries long-run deflation will prove to be the most effective way to attract foreign investment and meet competition in foreign markets. Under these conditions government bonds would show a constant tendency to rise above par and would be very attractive investments.

Under either of these two monetary environments, the government security can become an economically desirable investment. However, the problem of political stability and the possibility of repudiation or declaration of confiscation of the property of opposition groups remain. This difficulty will, of course, be diminished in time as a larger portion of the population becomes holders of government securities and as political maturity develops. Until this takes place, we have an opportunity for a new type of international fiscal agency.

This fiscal agency could guarantee the holders of approved government bonds from repudiation or confiscation. The cost of this insurance could be jointly shared by the community of nations and the issuing country. Of course, for a security to be approved, the terms would have to fit the nation's economic environment and the funds would have to be used for economic development.

I propose that the Bank of Korea take the initiative in proposing this type of an international agency.

Part II

TAXATION POLICIES
OF DEVELOPING NATIONS

Property Taxation Insights

*The next selection is taken from the October 1959
issue of The Punjab University Economist, published
in Pakistan.*

*The title "Property Taxation Insights" is broader
than justified by the analysis. Rather, it is a consideration of some of the relationships that seem to exist between property taxation and economic development.*

The property tax, which has enjoyed its greatest modern development in the United States, can be considered to be an expression of
our political and economic beliefs and realities. This seems to be generally true of a nation's tax system.

The famous salt tax (Gabelle) which formed a basic portion of the
revenue system of the Ancient Regime in France and the more ancient
empires of China[1] seems to have been an expression of the philosophies
and realities existing in those empires during their period of disorder
and decline.[2] The extensive use of sales taxes by the Soviet Union is
in accord with the Communist organization of production where the
State is the provider of the capital and is, of course, intimately involved in the productive process.[3]

United States Development

After the adoption of the Constitution and the completion of the
base of the political revolution, the people of the United States continued the revolution outlined in the Declaration of Independence by

[1] See the very interesting discussions of the use of China's ancient salt tax as
security for loans to China by Western nations before World War I. Esson M.
Gale, *Salt for the Dragon*, (East Lansing: Michigan State University Press,
1953), particularly pp. 100-106.

[2] When the governments of both France and China were strong, the taxation
of land provided the bulk of government revenues. In referring to China's land
tax, Han Liang Huang in *The Land Tax of China* (New York: Columbia University Press, 1918), p. 141, calls the land tax "this important source of national revenue which has almost from time immemorial been the main source of national
revenue."

[3] Franklin D. Holzman, *Soviet Taxation* (Cambridge: Harvard University
Press, 1955), pp. 87-99.

moving forward on the economic front. This development was most vividly shown in the rise of Jeffersonian and Jacksonian democracy. One very important economic effect of this was the elimination of the conservative European notion of exempting the property of the large landowners from whatever modified land taxes existed. This half-conscious political realization that democracy and the taxation of property were closely related was combined with Ricardian economics by the American publicist and economist, Henry George, in his famous book entitled *Progress and Poverty*.[4]

In this book Henry George showed that the increase in land values arose from increased productivity, which was closely related to the increase of population and wealth. He also showed through Ricardian-type rent analysis that this entire amount of income that gave land its value could be collected in taxes without decreasing the incentives for efficient production. This tax George called the "single tax" because he calculated that collections which he favored would be enough to cover all government expenditures, and because he thought that it would be the most socially desirable form of taxation.

On the other hand is Central and South America, where the economic revolution did not carry forward on the base of the political revolution, and where, as in Bolivia, "the land taxes on rural property made it easy to hold large tracts idle for prestige or speculative purposes."[5] It was not until 1920, and then in Mexico, a border nation, that a country south of the United States' border experienced a genuine economic revolution.[6] These related political and economic outgrowths are important in explaining the development of the taxation of real estate in the United States and the failure of the tax to develop in other areas where population growth was rapid and many land resources were underdeveloped.

Despite both an economic and political revolution in Mexico, the property tax provides less than 2 per cent of total tax revenue. In the primarily agricultural and land-based economy of India, land revenues are reported as 4 per cent of total tax revenues. In Turkey the portion of tax revenues arising from land taxes decreased from 7 per cent to 2 per cent between 1938 and 1949.[7] These countries undoubtedly possess a resource base that proved in the United States to be suitable to the use of the property tax. What they do not possess,

[4] Henry George, *Progress and Poverty* (New York: The Vanguard Press, 1929), pp. 59-64.

[5] United Nations Technical Assistance Administration, *Taxes and Fiscal Policy in Underdeveloped Countries* (New York, 1943), p. 47.

[6] James G. Maddox, *Mexican Land Reforms* (American Universities Field Staff Study, 1957).

[7] Arthur Robert Burns, *Comparative Economic Organization* (New York: Prentice-Hall, 1955), p. 697.

apparently, is the requisite economic and political climate for the development of this tax source.

Collection Trends

The United States entered into the twentieth century with the general property tax providing by far the largest portion of total tax collections. As late as 1932, the property tax provided over 50 per cent of the total tax collection of the federal, state, and local governments of the United States. However, the portion of tax collections arising from the property tax had already declined considerably by the 1920's. This decline continued steadily, although the absolute amount of property taxes collected has more than doubled since 1942. The increase has been from $4.3 billion in 1942 to about $12.0 billion in 1956.[8] This is a somewhat greater increase than the fall in the purchasing power of the dollar, and amounts to slightly more than 10 per cent of the overall total of tax collections in the United States.

The downward trend of the property tax as a source of government revenues has also been experienced in Japan, another country which has enjoyed a rapid economic growth and which also placed a major reliance on the property tax at an earlier date.[9] The national government of Japan was nearly completely dependent on revenues from the land tax from 1867 to the Sino-Japanese War of 1894-95. However, since that time to 1950 the decline was continuous. Since the new *Chiho-zei-ho*, the Local Tax Act of 1950, property tax collections have increased and they now constitute over 25 per cent of all prefectural, city, town, and village taxes.[10]

Property Tax Principles

Throughout the world, property taxation has been influenced by a number of economic concepts possessing important political overtones. The identification of these concepts and a very brief analysis is an important step forward toward the development of an understanding of the political and economic tug-of-war going on in all countries, for the property tax is always under consideration either as a greater or lesser source of tax revenues. The concepts are as follows:

Source of Land Value. The first concept relies to a very large extent, as we have seen above, on (what in the Western world has become

---

[8] Bureau of the Census, *Statistical Abstract of the United States, 1944-45* (Washington, D. C., Government Printing Office, 1945), Table 313, and *Summary of Government Finances in 1956*, p. 21.

[9] Hanya Ito, "Direct Taxes in Japan and the Shoup Report," *Public Finance*, vol. VIII, no. 4, 1953, pp. 358-359.

[10] Sabura Shiomi, *Japan's Finance and Taxation 1940-1956* (New York: Columbia University Press, 1947), p. 36.

associated with) the work of David Ricardo and Henry George. This concept considers the property tax as a levy on the land alone, and excludes from the base all improvements or permanent attachments that man has made to land. Under this concept of property taxation, the fundamental relationship is the widely accepted *social production* position, which is that value accruing to an individual, through no actual effort of that person, has been created by society and should be shared by society. This position epitomizes the thinking of Henry George.

Land as Cost. A second closely associated relationship used to support a property tax on land alone emphasizes that the market price of the products of land is determined by the cost of labor used in production, including capital equipment. Therefore, the amount remaining for distribution as rent is in excess. This excess is the payment made to the owners of the land; and because it is a surplus amount, it is not a necessary payment. It follows that the level of the tax placed upon land will not affect the price of products produced with the assistance of land, nor will it cause land to be withdrawn from productive activity. In fact, the impact is seen to be just the opposite, which makes a property tax based only on land a tax on economic surplus. This position finds its tap root in the economic writings of the classical economists.

Treatment of Buildings and Improvements. A third concept favoring inclusion of land alone in the property tax base is quite different and has both ancient and modern support. The position is: When the property tax includes in its base real estate other than land, and also personal tangible and intangible property, it acts to discourage investment and general improvement. Therefore, improvements on the land and other types of property should be excluded and only the value of the land itself should be included in the property tax base. In a recent study of the tax system of Jamaica completed by Professor J. R. and Mrs. U. K. Hicks,[11] this concept was partially adopted and also subjected to some criticism. Nevertheless, Jamaica has changed its property tax to correspond more closely to this concept.[12]

The special treatment of real estate improvements is the woof of the majority of the studies completed by Western-trained economists who analyze the tax systems of underdeveloped areas. The Hicks' study recommends exempting improvements to land for a limited number of years. The Chinese have generally felt that improvements should

[11] J. R. and U. K. Hicks, *Report on Finance and Taxation in Jamaica* (Kingston, Jamaica: Government Printer, 1955), p. 139.

[12] D. J. Morgan, "Land Valuation and Taxation in Jamaica," *Public Finance*, no. 3, 1957, pp. 232-238.

not be taxed.[13] The United Nations' experts, on the other hand, are somewhat doubtful of the advantages of exempting improvements to land. They point out that this procedure, particularly in the cities, stimulates speculative building and is likely to cause a misallocation of scarce investment funds.[14]

Another aspect of the question of excluding or including improvements and buildings in the land tax base is that of justice. The lands bearing large buildings and enjoying considerable improvements are frequently the lands which are also owned by wealthy persons.[15] Conversely, unimproved lands are frequently owned by persons lacking capital, which partially explains the unimproved nature of the land. The relationship of this situation to the requirements of a just distribution of the tax burden is too obvious for a government to overlook, especially a democratically oriented political regime.

Revenue on Cadastral (Capital Value) Base. Another basic aspect of the property tax is whether the tax should be levied on a cadastral basis or on a revenue basis. In Western Europe, the revenue or estimate of gross receipts from property was largely used as the base for the property tax. This procedure was carried over to underdeveloped areas under Western European influence.[16] For example, in 1926 a uniform land tax was adopted in Iran to supply the funds needed to support the army which was being used to bring the scattered tribes together into a nation. This land tax was "based on the gross produce."[17] The land tax in use in South Viet-Nam is a copy of the tax in France, and, when applied to rural areas, varies with the type of crop grown on the land and is limited to land producing an income.[18]

In Latin America, there is some revenue from land use as the base of the property tax, but land value as the base predominates; and the trend is in this direction. The land tax of Guatemala, for example, is based on the assessed value of real estate.[19]

The ancient property tax of China divided land into many categories and combined labor available to work the property (actually size of family) with the value set on the land in order to develop a com-

---

[13] Han Liang Huang, *op. cit.*, p. 170.

[14] See United Nations Technical Assistance Administration, *Taxes and Fiscal Policy in Underdeveloped Countries* (New York, 1954), p. 47.

[15] D. J. Morgan, *op. cit.*

[16] Jens Peter Jensen, *Property Taxation in the United States* (Chicago: The University of Chicago Press, 1931), p. 21.

[17] *Landlord and Peasant in Persia* (New York: Oxford University Press, 1953), p. 183.

[18] Ministre des Finances du Plan et de la Reconstruction, *Code National de l'impot Foncier, Etat du Viet-Nam* (Saigon, 1953).

[19] United Nations Technical Assistance Administration, *Taxes and Fiscal Policy in Underdeveloped Countries* (New York, 1954), p. 73.

bined land-labor tax on rural property. Thus, the property tax was more of a tax on the produce or gross receipts from the use of the land than a tax on the land itself.[20]

In Japan the taxation of rural land was based on assessed valuation, especially in the nineteenth century when the revenues played such an important role in economic development. By refusing to change either assessed valuations or the tax rate between 1881 and 1885 when prices in Japan were falling sharply, the Japanese finance minister was able to increase the government's real income. In this way he expanded the funds available to the government for use in subsidizing economic expansion.[21]

In Korea a tax in kind is levied on the basis of what is considered to be the average harvest. A commentator states: "This provision was intended to encourage heavier application of fertilizer and improved production methods."[22] In classification, this is a property tax base somewhere in between the cadastral and the revenue base. This compromise, officially or unofficially, is actually a very common situation. In Finland, for example, taxes follow an income basis, but this income is the average earned on the type of land the farmer owns and is computed on the basis of the three fiscal years preceding the taxation year. Under these conditions, a particularly efficient farmer bears no greater tax burden than an inefficient one.[23]

Relation of Principles to Applied Considerations

Whether the produce of land should be the base of taxation, or whether it should be the value of land under normal conditions, is a basic question in the consideration of land taxation. If the value of land is the base, a landowner pays the same tax whether or not he is completely and effectively using his land. Therefore, using production as the base makes it easier for a landowner to hold land idle as a speculation or as a prestige factor. This relationship is important in explaining the belief by many economic policy makers that the taxation of land on the cadastral basis is particularly useful where the productive use of land needs a stimulation.

Although the taxation of property, particularly in underdeveloped areas, is first associated with agriculture and rural life, these are not

---

[20] Han Liang Huang, op. cit., p. 168.

[21] Thomas C. Smith, *Political Change and Industrial Development in Japan: Government Enterprise, 1868-1880* (Stanford, California: Stanford University Press, 1955), p. 81.

[22] Haskell P. Wald, "Use of Tax Collections in Kind to Combat Inflation in the Republic of Korea," *Public Finance*, vol. IX, no. 2, 1954, p. 183.

[23] Lauri Kivivuori, "The Taxation of Farmers in Finland" (Helsinki: The Central Union of Agricultural Producers, 1955).

the limits of its applicability. Land values of urban areas increase rapidly together with the rising urban population. Speculative holding of idle city land under these conditions results in uneven and inefficient city development. Land taxation could substantially reduce speculative land holding while making substantial revenues available to the government.

Taxation in South Viet-Nam

This article is reprinted with permission from Public Finance, vol. XIV, no. 3-4, 1959, which is published in The Netherlands.

This is a summary of the tax system before and after reform efforts. Although the summary focuses on Viet-Nam, it provides an insight into the tax problems of all developing nations.

In South Viet-Nam the American military and economic aid programs are in intimate contact with the government administrative and economic institutional framework which the French leave behind in their colonial areas.[1] Because of this, taxation policies in President Ngo Dinh Diem's Viet-Nam transcend the importance of a purely Vietnamese or a Southeast Asian situation; it is a case study of the adaptability of a French-type tax system and French-trained tax officials in meeting the problems of a new nation.[2]

---

[1] South Viet-Nam is the name of international postal usage for the portion of Viet-Nam south of the 17th parallel. This area consists of three former administrative regions: south Viet-Nam, central Viet-Nam, and the plateau area. The population of this area was 12,261,000 in 1955 as given in the *Annuaire Statistique du Viet-Nam*, 1956, pp. 36-43. The per capita income at the official rate of exchange was $144 in 1955. *Bulletin Economique de la Banque National du Viet-Nam*, no. 2, 1956, p. 24.

[2] National tax legislation in effect up to 1957 amendments is included in four publications prepared by the Ministers des Finances des Plan et de la Reconstruction published in Saigon on 1 April 1953. The 1957 amendments are available in a mimeographed translation dated March 1957. This was prepared by the economic section of the Viet-Nam National Institute of Administration in Saigon.

South Viet-Nam's new constitution of 1956 does not contain detailed provisions relative to taxation. In an analysis of this constitution, J. A. C. Grant fails to mention any fiscal provisions in "The Viet-Nam Constitution of 1956," *American Political Science Review*, June 1958, pp. 437-462.

Articles 43 and 61 are concerned with finance. Article 43 provides for the presentation of the budget by the President. The term is obviously used to include both revenue sources and expenditures. Article 61 states "Deputies have the right to initiate expenditures but at the same time they shall propose corresponding new receipts." Apparently the assumption of the framers of the constitution was that the executive will exercise greater fiscal responsibility than the assembly. Also it seems to limit the assembly tax powers to the initiation of new taxes to cover the cost of new legislative enactments.

This justification for the analysis of the tax system of a new nation is really not needed as *raison d'être*, for today the problem of developing ways for new nations to become fiscally viable has gained a high priority on the list of worthwhile areas in fiscal research.

The taxes of South Viet-Nam are closely modeled after the French tax system of about forty years ago. The name of the tax, the tax base, and the tax rates are often identical with those at present or formerly in use in France.[3]

However, in the past these taxes were largely collected from the French community and were not generally applied to the Vietnamese and Chinese residents. The taxes collected from the indigenous population arose from a partially clandestine opium monopoly and a highly developed legal prostitution and gambling industry. Today the French community is much smaller; and opium, gambling, and prostitution are illegal. This has put the French tax system as it has been transplanted to South Viet-Nam to the test. The test is whether this tax system can be used to collect from the natives of South Viet-Nam the quantities of revenue required to support a government and to provide some capital for economic development.

This paper is a summary of the tax system of South Viet-Nam, a consideration of the effectiveness of this system under today's changed conditions, and an analysis of the tax legislation initiated by President Diem's government in 1957.

Customs

The tax revenues of South Viet-Nam are dominated by customs and regie (additional excise tax levied on selected imported and domestic

---

[3] The following two translations from the Saigon Press, the first the Chinese Press and the second the Vietnamese Press, describe typical types of tax problems encountered by new governments.

Viet Hoa, 20 November 1956: "News received from the authorities discloses that after completion of the general census of all foreigners living in the territory of South Viet-Nam, the Vietnamese Government will increase taxes for foreign residents. This step aims at making a difference of payment of taxes between foreigners and Vietnamese.

"According to the authorities, the exacting of high taxes from foreigners has been a common practice in other nations. However, foreigners who have obtained Vietnamese citizenship are not required to pay these high taxes."

Tin Dien, 26 December 1956: "Recently an embezzlement of some one million piasters was discovered at the Excise Administration Service in Cholon, the culprit being the secretary in charge of receipts, Tang Canh Dinh.

"Dinh's practice consisted in registering on the receipt book counterfoil only part of the sums paid in fines or taxes, keeping the rest for himself. The theft was discovered when the Finance Inspector found some differences between the amounts on the receipts Dinh had delivered to taxpayers and the counterfoils.

"Dinh and two other secretaries of the Service have been arrested and questioned by the Security Service."

goods). Nearly two thirds of the total customs and regie collections are levied on imports (some customs collections arise from exports— primarily rubber). This, however, is not all the tax revenues that are collected directly from imports. Table 1 provides an estimate of the total tax collections directly related to imports. The total is 3,559,185,-000 piasters.[4] In the same year tax collections totaled 5,856,939,000 piasters. Thus in 1955 imports were the base for about 60 per cent of the tax collections of the national government. The tax legislation of 1957 increased tax collections by some 15 per cent. This development resulted in an increase in the portion of tax collections based on imports.[5]

TABLE 1

TAX REVENUES ARISING DIRECTLY
FROM SOUTH VIET-NAM'S IMPORTS, 1955
(IN THOUSANDS OF PIASTERS)

Type of Tax	Amount
Import duties	1,509,961
General interior tax	471,211
Regie on gasoline and kerosene	336,092
¾ of miscellaneous customs and regie	270,632
¾ of turnover tax	621,352
½ of patente (business license tax)	109,302
½ of income tax on individual and corporation profits	231,306
Total	3,549,856

An unusual feature of South Viet-Nam's imports, and therefore of the fiscal situation of the national government, is that about 73 per cent of the imports are financed with American aid.[6] Also, nearly all the imports into South Viet-Nam have been purchased with foreign exchange acquired at the official rate of exchange ($275,673,000 piasters, official rate, are not). This procedure has meant that imports are purchased at about one half the world price. Put differently, the present procedure provides a 115 per cent subsidy to importers; the importer can purchase for 35 piasters on the official market what on the free market would cost 75 piasters. This underpricing of imports has given the purchasers of imports an immense ability to bear taxes. The collection of high taxes on imports under these circumstances could be

---

[4] The official value of the piaster is 35 to the dollar and 1 to 10 francs. The rate on what might best be described as the free market is about 70 piasters to the dollar.

[5] These reforms are discussed later in this paper. About 90 per cent of total tax collections are national government taxes.

[6] Banque Nationale du Viet-Nam, *Balance Generale des Paiements du Viet-Nam en 1955* (Saigon, 1956), pp. 17-19.

considered to be a method of indirectly bringing about a devaluation of the piaster. Despite this unusually favorable situation relative to the real burden of taxation in South Viet-Nam, tax collections were estimated to be 7.5 per cent of gross national product in 1956.[7]

Turnover Tax

Until March 1957, the second most important source of tax revenues was the turnover tax *(chiffre d'affaire)*. The tax was originally introduced in 1947 at a 1 per cent rate. Since 1 May 1953 the rate has been 4 per cent. The additional 3 per cent tax is called the *surtaxe d'armement*, and the revenues were to be used to support the war effort. Both the *chiffre d'affaire* and the *surtaxe d'armament* were repealed in March 1957.

The base of the tax was very broad and included services (except professional such as dentist and lawyer services) and all sales of goods except the original sale by the producer of farm products. The tax was levied on each transaction, making a theoretical tax of 12 to 16 per cent. However, the tax was badly enforced as indicated by the 1955 collections of 929,344,000 piasters. This total is only about 10 per cent of the CIF price of imported goods and perhaps less than 4 per cent of the retail price of imported goods alone (CIF price plus customs duties plus mark-ups), and much less than 2 per cent of taxable transactions."[8] As Table 1 indicates, about three fourths of the 1955 collections are properly allocated as a tax on imported goods.

Production Tax

The production tax was introduced in 1957 as a replacement for the turnover tax. The new tax was seen to be a procedure of 1) increasing tax collections without increasing the legal tax burden, 2) reducing tax evasion and tax personnel corruption temptation, and 3) making the distribution of the tax burden correspond more closely to ability to pay.

---

[7] For a summary of a confidential study of Viet-Nam's tax system, see *Summary of Principles and Recommendations Included in R. W. Lindholm's "Analysis of Viet-Nam's Tax System"* prepared for ICA by Henry Tenenbaum, Deputy Chief, USOM Finance Division (Saigon, 6 August 1956).

[8] The gross national product of South Viet-Nam was estimated to be 80 billion piasters in 1954. If it is assumed that the amount of GNP arising from consuming one's own production or bartering is equal to the difference between GNP and the transaction total, the rate is 1.2 per cent. The CIF (free market rate) value of imports is, on the basis of this comparison, about 25 per cent of GNP. Calculated from Banque Nationale du Viet-Nam, *Estimations du Revenue National du Viet-Nam en 1954* (Saigon, 1956).

Actually the new production tax provided for the repeal of three taxes: the general interior tax on imports, the general interior tax on local products, and the turnover tax, which included the surcharge for armament.

At the high level of imports prevailing in 1956, the interior tax on imports provided about 350,000,000 piasters of revenues. This was somewhat more than a third as much as was collected from the turnover tax and its armament surcharge. The rates of the general interior tax on imported goods were 4, 6, and 10 per cent depending on the good imported. If the good was a basis for further production the rate was the minimum; if it was a luxury good the rate was likely to be the maximum. The interior tax on domestically produced goods was unimportant and provided only about 8,000,000 piasters of tax revenues.

Therefore the effect of the production tax, with its rates of 15, 20, or 35 per cent on imported goods, was to bring a somewhat reduced theoretical tax burden on imports of consumption necessities and goods used in further production that were sold through normal distribution channels. It somewhat increased the burden on luxury goods and goods not necessary in carrying out normal economic functions. The tax on goods of domestic production at a rate of 6 per cent reduces the taxes considerably on goods produced under conditions that make them subject to the tax. Previously these goods, marketed through normal trade channels, would be theoretically subject to a tax rate of 12 or 18 per cent of the processor's sale price.

For those domestic goods exempted from the production tax, the reform eliminated the legal tax burden by the full amount of the turnover and armament tax plus the interior tax on domestically produced goods. The production tax base excludes the production of producers 1) employing less than six workers including members of family, 2) using only simple machines that are relatively unimportant in the production process, and 3) having annual sales that total less than 500,000 piasters (about $14,000 at the official rate of exchange).

Although the goods produced under conditions making them exempt from the production tax make up an unknown but very substantial portion of the total production of South Viet-Nam, they had not provided an important portion of the actual tax base. Thus, this exemption did not bring about a substantial narrowing of the tax base which had been available to the turnover tax and the interior tax on domestically produced goods.

The introduction of the production tax has substantially increased revenues and seems very likely to have caused a general improvement in the effectiveness of South Viet-Nam's tax administration. However, the large collections that have been experienced are dependent upon continued large imports and somewhat upon the continued overvaluation of the piaster. Both of these are in turn closely related to the amount of foreign aid South Viet-Nam receives. The reform failed to make any substantial progress toward shifting the tax system from one based on foreign economic activity to a tax system based on the principal economic base of the Vietnamese agricultural production.[9]

Income Tax

For practical purposes the income tax of South Viet-Nam consists of four parts, but the law provides for nine separate *cedulaires,* or types of income. The four parts are as follows:

1. The tax upon income other than wage income, which is taxed at 16 per cent if it is the income of an unincorporated business and 24 per cent if it is the income of an incorporated business. Over 90 per cent of the collections of this portion of the income tax arise from assessments on corporate income.

2. The tax on salary and wage income with a rate from 1 to 5 per cent.

3. The general income tax which is applied to wage and salary income and all other income of natural persons (including distributed corporate profits) with rates from 1 to 50 per cent. This tax is applied in practice to the same base as the income tax on wages and salaries and the other income of natural persons.

These three income taxes are administered by the Direction of Direct Taxes, which is a part of the General Direction of Taxation. The other important operating division of the General Direction is the Direction of Indirect Taxes. About 80 per cent of the total collections from these three income taxes arise from the 24 per cent rate, which is applied to corporate income. The collections from the income tax on salaries and wages were only about 544,230 piasters in 1955 and the collections from the general income tax were 83,052,000 piasters.[10]

---

[9] In mid-1958 Cambodia, which as a part of French Indo-China had a tax system identical to that of South Viet-Nam, modified its tax system along the lines adopted in South Viet-Nam in 1957. In Cambodia, however, the turnover tax was continued in a modified form. Under the new legislation the tax is applied only on the first sale of a product.

[10] The very small collection from the income tax on salaries and wages arises to a considerable extent from the failure of the Secretary of Finance to use the power he possesses to initiate withholding of income taxes from salaries. This situation forced the tax administration to place the following item in all the principal newspapers of Saigon on 14 January 1957:

"The Directorate for Tax asks all public and private offices, individuals, and mutual associations to send in before January 31 statements of all payments made during 1956 such as salaries, allowances, bonuses to employees, salaries to members of any board, business commissions, royalties to writers and inventors,

4. The last income tax is levied on interest and dividends paid out by corporations and is administered by the Direction of Registration, which is a part of the Department of Finance, but is not under the General Direction of Taxation as is the regular corporate income tax. The rate of this tax is 18 per cent on SARL (private) corporations and 24 per cent on SA (public) corporations; three fourths of the collections arise from SARL corporations. The collections from this income tax are slightly less than half the collections from the regular corporate income tax and more than twice the total collections from taxes applied to the income of natural persons. In 1955 the total collections from these four income taxes were 744,500,000 piasters, or not quite 13 per cent of the total tax revenues available to the national government.[11]

The three income taxes under the Direction of Direct Taxes are assessed but are not collected by this Direction. The actual collection is carried out by the Treasury, which is a part of the Department of Finance, but possesses a very independent status and is not controlled in any way by the Direction of Direct Taxes. The tax on distributed earnings and interest paid by corporations is both assessed and collected by the Direction of Registration, which is also a part of the Department of Finance but is not under the General Direction of Taxes—and is therefore quite separate from the Direction of Direct Taxes.

The tax burden on corporate net income is rather high. For example, the net income of a public (SA) corporation distributing all its earnings in dividends, with the dividends being received by stockholders on the average in the 15 per cent general income tax bracket, would bear a 52 per cent tax. The total general income tax collections of 83,098,000 piasters indicate that most of the dividends do not get included under the general income tax.[12]

Registration

The taxes collected by the Direction of Registration *(droits d'Enregistrement)* are related to property transfers and documents of property ownership. The collections totaled 589,293,000 piasters in 1955, in-

---

retirement funds or pensions. This statement must be made on forms provided by the Direct Tax Service."

The response (1956 income year collection) was not great, although through other administrative devices it was possible to show some improvement.

[11] South Viet-Nam was originally (1955) divided into three regions. Since 1956 these regional divisions have been gradually eliminated. In 1956, for fiscal purposes, the regions were combined with the national government.

[12] Data on the composition of the general income tax base showed that 21.84 per cent of the taxable base arise from income of securities held.

cluding the tax on corporate dividend and interest payments referred
to above.

The transfer of ownership of real estate property is taxed at 13.2
per cent of the value of the sale if the property has been sold one or more
times since 1948 and 18 per cent if the first sale has been since 1948.
The tax rate on automobile sales is 3.6 per cent if under 15 horsepower and 9.0 per cent if over 15 horsepower.[13]

The death taxes of South Viet-Nam produce very little revenue
and consist only of an inheritance tax. The tax exempts Vietnamese
inheritances under 50,000 piasters and allows 20 per cent of the total
estate to be set aside to celebrate death anniversaries. The tax has a
different and higher rate structure for French and other foreign inhabitants than for Vietnamese. The tax rates vary from 2 per cent to 48 per
cent of the inheritance.

The stamp tax legislation requires a stamp be attached to every
conceivable type of official and legal document. In 1955 the stamp tax
on checks was removed. The cost of administering the stamp taxes appears to be about 20 per cent of collections, while in 1955 the average
cost of administering all taxes collected by the Direction of Registration was 4.2 per cent.

The insurance tax is a tax on premiums and varies from 3.84 per
cent of life insurance premiums to 16.60 per cent of fire insurance premiums.

The registration taxes, particularly those on debt documents, are
undoubtedly a burden to commerce. The tax rate on loan contracts is
1.2 per cent of the value of the contract and does not vary with the
length of the contract or the rate of interest. Actually the tax is only
paid if court action is contemplated.

Special Excise Taxes

The special excise taxes are becoming more productive through
increased administrative effort, higher rates, and the expansion of the
coverage. In all instances these taxes include the idea of special taxation of luxury consumption, particularly of imported or Western-type
goods. Another element involved in the selection of the goods and
services subject to special taxation has been the possibility of effective
administration. However, in the case of taxes administered by the
General Direction of Taxation, ease of administration does not appear
to have been a dominant element.

The special excise taxes are divided into two administrative groupings, those administered by the General Direction of Taxation and
those administered under regie. This division is one arising from the

---

[13] European concept of horsepower.

historical development of tax administration in France and is not particularly based upon administrative desirability or economic usefulness in South Viet-Nam.

Special excise taxes administered by the General Direction of Taxation are as follows: paddy (rice) transformation tax, meat consumption tax, ice consumption tax, entertainment tax, luxury tax on precious metals, luxury tax on consumption in restaurants, gasoline and other petroleum products tax.

The regie taxes are administered through a division of the Customs Service, and here ease of administration appears to have been more important. However, the twin concepts of luxury consumption and the consumption of Western-type goods continue to be important. Another element which has caused certain products to be taxed under regie has been the former or present manufacture of these products by the French government.

These taxes have been imposed on 13 different commodities, such as gasoline, cigarettes, alcohol including wine and beer, matches, mineral oils, radio tubes, gun powder, fireworks, salt, and sugar. About 50 per cent of the collections from taxes administered under regie arise from the tax on cigarettes and approximately another 30 per cent from the tax on gasoline and kerosene. Gasoline is included as a product subject to special taxation under both the Direction of Indirect Taxation and regie. The revenues in both cases go into the general fund.

Real Estate Tax

The taxation of real estate is divided into three categories: rice land, agricultural land used for other purposes, and urban land and buildings.[14] In addition to the revenues available to the regions from taxing the first two categories of real estate and now available to the national government, the provinces, villages, and cities are permitted to add a percentage which varies from 200 per cent of the national tax for urban land in Saigon to 5 per cent additional tax on rice land for the village budget and 10 per cent additional tax on rice land for the provincial budget. The tax is administered theoretically by the national government, but because the assessors outside the capital are appointed by local provincial chiefs, the national government's control is very weak beyond the Saigon metropolitan area. The tax has not been a large revenue raiser, and collections have been less than 1 per cent of total national tax receipts.

---

[14] The traditional Chinese-type land tax used in ancient Viet-Nam possessed a number of features similar to the French system. See Han Liang Huang, "The Land Tax in China," *Studies in History, Economics and Public Law*, vol. 80 (New York: Columbia University Press, 1918).

The failure of the Vietnamese tax system to collect significant revenues from domestic activities is a basic weakness.[15] More than likely a successful land tax program is the *conditio sine qua non* for an adequate government revenue system in Viet-Nam.

Patente

The patente is a business license tax based on the type of business and the estimate of the rental value of the premises occupied. In addition, selected businesses are taxed on the basis of gross receipts of the previous year. Here again the local governments are permitted to add a given percentage to the basic tax (the amount permitted is 200 per cent, plus 2.5 per cent for the Vietnamese Chamber of Commerce, and if a Chinese business, an additional 15 per cent for the Chinese Chamber of Commerce). The revenues produced by the basic patente rate were formerly available to the regional government; they were transferred to the national government in 1953.

Summary and Conclusions

The tax system of Viet-Nam makes very little use of direct taxes. The income tax produces some revenues, but nearly all are collected from corporations. The real estate tax produces very little revenue outside of the Saigon metropolitan area. The taxes on business, such as many of those collected by registration, and the patente and the former turnover tax were subject to wide abuse because of a faulty base and a rate structure that was not expected to be generally fully applied. The tax system fails to collect significant revenues from basic domestic activities and instead is aimed at the taxation of imports and Western-type consumption goods, i.e., cigarettes and gasoline, which can be doubtfully labeled luxury goods.

This is a picture of a weak tax system. The ordinary tax revenues in 1955 were down 453,128,000 piasters from the 1954 level. This decrease in revenues took place while prices were rising by approximately 10 per cent and commercial importers were enjoying a very substantial subsidy. Comparable tax collection data of 1955 and 1956 show a continued downward trend (collections of major national government taxes for the first five months of 1956 were down 10 per cent from 1955) while prices continued to rise. The adoption of the production tax in 1957 plus other additional taxes on luxury goods and

---

[15] In this respect South Viet-Nam is not alone among the new nations. Between 1938 and 1950 the portion of total taxes arising from taxes assessed upon property decreased in India, Brazil, Egypt, Iran, Syria, and Turkey. See Arthur Robert Burns, *Comparative Economic Organization* (New York: Prentice-Hall, 1955), p. 697.

gasoline plus tax administration developments caused the tax collection trend to reverse itself. This development certainly deserves commendation. However, until the government of South Viet-Nam is able to make substantial collections from its basic agricultural production activities, it has not turned the fiscal viability corner.

Land Use and Land Taxation Policies of Non-Communist Underdeveloped Areas

This article is reprinted with permission from the April 1960 issue of Economic Development and Cultural Change, *which is published and copyrighted by the University of Chicago Press in Illinois.*

Professor Lindholm gives a concise consideration of why land taxation has not become an important revenue source in the developing nations of the free world. He concludes that the failure to do so can only mean victory for communism.

The property tax was extensively used and proved to be very productive in the United States and Japan during their periods of transition from an agricultural to an industrial economic base. This similarity of tax policy during a period of rapid introduction of industrial processes was the case, although population density and other conditions related to land use were very different in the two countries.[1]

Despite the demonstrated productivity of the land tax as a source of government revenues in underdeveloped and non-Communist areas and its proven compatibility with industrial progress, the tax is not extensively used by the democratic low-per-capita-income countries.[2]

[1] U.S. Department of Commerce, Bureau of the Census, *Statistical Abstract of the United States;* Richard W. Lindholm, *Public Finance and Fiscal Policy* (New York, 1950), pp. 407-410; Thomas C. Smith, *Political Change and Industrial Development in Japan: Government Enterprise, 1868-1880* (Stanford, California, 1955); and "The Land Tax in the Tokugawa Period," *The Journal of Asian Studies*, pp. 3-19.

[2] "In many underdeveloped countries, taxes on land, agricultural produce, or agricultural income take a smaller share of farm income and represent a smaller proportion of the government revenue than they did before the Second World

Since the days when the property tax provided the major revenue source in agricultural United States and Japan, the world has been blanketed by Communist-type propaganda. An important aspect of this propaganda is the promise of land to the peasant when Communists control the government. This prospect seems to appeal to a fundamental desire of peasants everywhere.[3] This attitude can perhaps be traced to folktales telling of the idyllic life of the landowner.[4]

The governments of underdeveloped areas in the free world feel that they must counter the Communist appeal by also offering the peasant land. However, the non-Communist countries cannot just take ("expropriate") the lands, as can the Communists. Therefore, non-Communist countries establish a procedure to compensate landlords. The scheme usually involves the issuance of bonds.[5]

The government of an underdeveloped nation carrying out a land reform (breaking up land holdings into small ownership units) has no practical way of retiring and meeting interest payments on the bonds issued to former landlords except to collect annual payments from the multitude of new peasant proprietors.[6] To the new peasant landlord these payments are very similar to the former rent payments. In fact they may be more difficult to meet, for the government, in case of peasant adversity, is likely to be less understanding than was the landlord. Also, many governments are likely to be rather ineffec-

War." United Nations, Department of Economic Affairs, *Progress in Land Reform* (New York, 1954), p. 267. In Bolivia "the land taxes (because of low rates) on rural property make it easy to hold large tracts idle for prestige or speculative purposes." United Nations, Technical Assistance Administration, *Taxes and Fiscal Policy in Underdeveloped Countries* (New York, 1953), p. 47. In Turkey the portion of the tax revenues arising from land taxes decreased from 7 per cent to 2 per cent between 1938 and 1949. Arthur Burns, *Comparative Economic Organization* (New York, 1955), p. 697. Also see H. Wald, ed., *Agricultural Taxation and Economic Development* (Cambridge, 1954).

[3] "The overwhelming majority of the peasants, i.e., all except the rich ones who retain the tail of feudalism, positively demand 'land to the tillers.'" Seventh National Congress of the Chinese Communist Party, a political report made "On Coalition Government," Mao Tse-tung, *Selected Works* (New York, 1956, vol. 4, 1941-1945), p. 292. See also Naum Jasny, *The Socialized Agriculture of the USSR* (Stanford, California, 1949), pp. 5-6; and James G. Maddox, *Land Reform in Mexico* (New York, 1950), p. 1.

[4] Alvin Johnson, "The Communist Farmer," *Social Research,* vol. 25, no. 2, p. 228.

[5] Sometimes payment is made partly in cash and partly as investment in industry, as in Taiwan. On occasion the bonds are payable in kind rather than in money. For an analysis and description of many programs, see Kenneth H. Parsons, Raymond J. Penn, and Philip M. Raup, eds., *Land Tenure* (Madison, Wisconsin, 1956).

[6] This at least has appeared to be the case. For an analysis of this possibility, see Martin Bronfenbrenner, "The Appeal of Confiscation in Economic Development," *Economic Development and Cultural Change,* pp. 201-219. See also footnote 14

tive in providing technical and financial assistance to improve production and marketing techniques.[7] The net result is very likely to
be high cost agricultural production, continued grinding peasant
poverty, and disorganization of the agricultural sector.[8]

Before the days of the Communist programs and propaganda, money
lenders, landlords, speculators, and other groups small in total numbers
but strong economically had to rely on their own political power to
prevent the government from using agricultural land as an important base of taxation. Communist propaganda has greatly improved
the political position of these groups. Today they can very effectively
raise the Communist bogey when land taxation is considered. They
raise their voices along with the Communist agitators to point out
that land taxation will make the lot of the poor tiller and new landowner even more difficult.[9] The effect is to place the masses in the
rural areas of non-Communist countries on the side of the speculators, middlemen, and landowners. So the governments of non-Communist underdeveloped areas are very hesitant to use their land taxation powers.[10]

[7] See Lowry Nelson, *Land Reform in Italy* (Washington, 1956), p. 29.

[8] The basic and often neglected point of land reform is that it should be aimed
at elimination of inefficiency. Sometimes this inefficiency is great, frenquently it is
not. For example, the United Nations, *Economic Survey of Latin America, 1955*,
p. 48, states: "Production increments of sugar cane attained by Peru in the last
few years have mainly been derived from better unit yields, thanks to the adoption
of modern cultivation techniques. . . . The degree of efficiency in processing and
the higher yields allow Peruvian sugar to compete on the world market without
state protection." See also report of U.N. Economic Commission for Latin America, 1959, *New York Times,* 19 May 1959.

[9] It is reported that in India land taxation is not used to assist in land reform
because it is believed ". . . the burden would be passed on by the absentee land-
holder to the cultivating tenant." United Nations, Department of Economic and
Social Affairs, *Progress in Land Reform*, Second Report (New York, 1956), p.
115.

[10] "Land revenue contributes only about 8 per cent of total tax revenues of
India.

"Doubtless India's land taxes could be raised somewhat, especially on lands
improved by the government through irrigation and so on. This the states are
doing to some extent. It is expected that, with land reform, the contribution of
land and agriculture can be increased." Government of India, Planning Commission, *The New India* (New York, 1958), pp. 138-139.

"Private landowners pay no tax on their property in land, and the income tax
is not progressive. The new control of Iraq's water and land will thus serve to
increase the incomes of a class which now contributes little to development and
which is opposed to social progress." Doreen Warriner, *Land Reform and Development in the Middle East* (Garden City, England, 1957), p. 135.

"The land tax which was an important source of revenue in the countries of
the Middle East and Latin America has lost its revenue significance in all these
countries. Contributions from this source do not exceed one tenth of total tax
receipts in most of them." *Economic Bulletin for Asia and the Far East,* vol. IX,
no. 1, p. 3.

The initiation of land reform seriously limits the fiscal choices of non-Communist governments of underdeveloped countries. The action largely eliminates the possibility of using the property tax as a major revenue source in the near future.[11] This makes it difficult for these governments to collect the funds required for normal operations and next to impossible to finance expansion of productivity with tax revenues. This squeeze is very likely to result in deficit government finance, which will develop inflationary pressures and reduce the effectiveness of the taxes being utilized.[12]

Deficit finance and inflation, which are made nearly inevitable by land reform, reduce the value of the bonds and money payments received by the former landlords. If the inflation is very rapid, as it tends to be, compensated land reform approaches very close to land expropriation. To attempt to reduce the deterioration of the purchasing power of money unit contracts by increasing the payments to the new peasant proprietors will develop new political difficulties arising from the "money illusion" and will not directly improve the government's fiscal situation nor the rate of economic development. To make the sales contract in terms of rice, as was done in Taiwan, or in terms of some other produce, introduces additional rigidities in land usage that are highly undesirable.

More than likely the most undesirable aspect of non-Communist underdeveloped nation's adopting land reform is that the resulting land ownership fragmentation will make the adoption of modern agricultural production methods more difficult to organize and finance, and perhaps uneconomical. The Communists avoid this serious deficiency of fragmentation by initiating the second step of their program of reorganizing the agricultural sector. This is, of course, the large state-controlled and managed collective farms or communes, where the former peasants become laborers. The best procedure open to the non-Communist nation wishing to benefit from "big-scale farming with machinery," while enjoying land reform, is to organize cooperatives.

---

[11] "It cannot, however, be denied that the present systems of agricultural taxation offer a wide scope for improvement. . . . Taxation of land on the basis of capital value and in the form of a property tax *in rem* may have other advantages which deserve thorough examination by governments in the region." United Nations, Secretariat of the Economic Commission for Asia and the Far East, "Taxation and Development of Agriculture in Underdeveloped Countries, with Special Reference to Asia and the Far East," *Economic Bulletin for Asia and the Far East,* vol. IX, pp. 9-10.

[12] Latin America, for example, has suffered from "chronic inflation"; and it has also been true that property taxes and direct internal taxes generally have provided minimal revenues. United Nations, *Economic Survey of Latin America, 1955* (New York, 1956), pp. 131-151.

This method of organizing agricultural production is difficult and has not proved to be particularly attractive or efficient.[13]

Land reform through partial confiscation of privately owned land weakens citizen faith in government protection of contract rights;[14] fragments agricultural production units; eliminates the principal, and maybe the most desirable, government revenue possibility;[15] makes deficit government finance inevitable; and nearly necessitates the initiation of extensive direct government economic controls. In each instance, the direct impact and private and government reaction is unfavorable to rapid economic development of a non-Communist nation.

The "land reform" approach to land management and land use in non-Communist underdeveloped countries causes a destruction of institutional relationships, of political power balances, and of production bases which seem to be necessary for a rapid economic development along democratic lines. This danger is sufficiently imminent and important to warrant careful consideration by free world economic strategists.

---

[13] See Alta Ullah, *The Co-operative Movement in the Punjab* (London, 1937); Sir Alan Pim, *Colonial Agricultural Production* (London, 1946), pp. 10-11; and Charles P. Kindleberger, *Economic Development* (New York, 1958), p. 231.

[14] "The outright expropriation of large landowners in favor of their tenants also gives the beneficiaries a breathing-space and easement which may yield higher output. But the disadvantages are likely to be even greater. . . . In particular the disregard of property rights is likely to weaken confidence throughout the economy at large, and to discourage capital formation. . . ." Peter T. Bauer and Basil S. Hamey, *The Economics of Underdeveloped Countries* (Chicago, 1957), pp. 212-213.

[15] "The present administrative machinery for land revenue assessment in many countries should be able to cope with land value assessments with only slight adjustments. Taxation of land on the basis of capital value can also facilitate the assessment and administration of death duties and levies on wealth or net worth taxation which are receiving increased attention on the part of the governments in Asia and the Far East." United Nations, *Economic Bulletin for Asia and the Far East,* vol. IX, no. 1, p. 10. See also Haskel B. Wald, *Taxation of Agricultural Land in Underdeveloped Economies* (Cambridge, 1959), p. 184.

Political Role
of Taxation

*This selection is taken from Professor Lindholm's
study of the tax system of Viet-Nam. Here he departs
from the usual "economic" analysis of taxation to show
the "social" impact of widely distributed taxation.*

Taxation is an important economic area of both study and action
and is intimately interwoven with practical politics and the grand concepts of political theorists. The emphasis in this section is on the usefulness of taxes in developing a national unit and a responsible, efficient, democratic government.

Taxation, which in the world of yesterday was a means of financing luxurious spending by the court favorites, has become in the democratic world of today a method of group financing of projects for the
general welfare. The magic key to the transformation of taxes from
a symbol of oppression to a symbol of group cooperation is popular
control over expenditures and methods of finance. Therefore, taxation in the political and economic sense cannot be separated from government expenditure. What is important here is that taxation to perform the political function of creating a spirit of oneness must be the
result of group discussion on how to provide funds to finance projects
that the citizens wish to enjoy.

This "development of group feeling" function of taxation can be
made specific. For example: if the State Secretary for Education
wishes to build a school in a particular village, he goes to the national Treasurer and is given the funds. These funds have been provided to the Treasurer by the central bank through an expansion of
the money supply ... thus the school becomes something provided
by a rich uncle. The more cynical members of the village will see the
construction of the school as a way of buying their support or maybe
as a way of increasing the wealth of a relative of the State Secretary who is in the contracting business. To others, it is evidence that
the great State Secretary is thinking of even a poor village; and they
are appreciative and thankful as beneficiaries of the government's
bounty. Other reactions would be expected, but the feeling that the

school was a village accomplishment which had been made possible as a result of their working together would not be one of them. If, however, the school building was financed through both monetary and in-kind payments provided through village taxation, the school would be the result of group accomplishment, the object of group pride, and its destruction a group loss.

In short, a basic political principle of taxation is "local taxes for local projects locally determined." This does not mean the national government does not collect taxes or is not involved in the financing of local projects—far from it. For example, the national government might provide the radios, technical equipment, and trained personnel for the schools from its revenues. Also, the national government might supervise local revenue procedures to assure justice; and it might introduce new ideas into the village and, in this way, change the villagers' wants.

In addition to their parochial needs, the people of Viet-Nam have national desires and aspirations, which best achieve national unity. But these desires only become a part of the people's culture when their nationalistic activities are financed through taxes collected by the government through power granted by people who believe the activities to be a wise use of *their* income. Under these conditions, a modern medical school becomes an institution to serve the people; and they, because they paid for it, have the right to be certain it performs the services desired.

Another political aspect of taxation is its relationship to honesty in government. Popular confidence in a government and popular support of a government are closely related to government honesty. Honesty in government is, of course, closely related to effective accounting and budgeting procedures; but, in addition to these administrative "temptation reducers," government honesty requires the interest of the ordinary citizen. Citizen receipt of the tax bill has always been an excellent creator of interest in what is happening to government revenues. Borrowing from the central bank or collecting taxes indirectly does not bring the tax bill into existence, and honesty in government is certain to suffer. The reduction of government honesty correspondingly reduces popular confidence in and support of the government.

The impact of the tax bill is an example of a sound economic and political principle of taxation—the wide use of direct taxes. Direct taxation involves the use of a tax bill; the taxpayer is fully aware of paying taxes. Therefore, direct taxation develops the maximum impact in the development of government honesty.

Another sound economic principle of taxation is that the burden should be widely diffused. The wide diffusion should not only arise indirectly through the tax's incidence, but also directly through payments to the Treasurer. A sound political principle here is the prevention of a government supported by the few that is a government for only the few.

There is another taxation principle discussed at considerable length in this study which is associated with the above political point of "control of government by the large taxpayers." It is the economic principle that tax payments are not voluntary contributions which can be withheld at will. To perform the economic function allocated to taxation, the tax administration staff must be sufficiently numerous and skilled to force payments into the Treasury. The political point here is that a sound tax administration prevents political blackmail of the government.

Governments tend to be extravagant, partly because of varied and insistent pressures and partly because they (the executive branch) are spending someone else's money. A government cannot generally use the test of profitability of an additional expenditure as can a business firm. The influences affecting government expenditure vary from the provision of national security to taking care of good old Vinh. The best control, both politically and economically, is the requirement that what is voted to be spent must also be collected in taxes from the general population, and in some instances, collected from those most directly benefiting from the expenditure.

Politically, the requirement of raising in taxes what is spent restrains spending because the voters favoring the expenditure are somewhat offset by voters who will be required to pay higher taxes due to the spending. Economically, it corresponds somewhat to the "compensating principle" developed by a number of American fiscal economists. The principle, briefly stated, is that a government expenditure should be made if the total additional benefit units from the expenditure outweigh the total of additional sacrifice units arising from the transfer of additional funds to the government.

This discussion has been gradually and cautiously approaching the nub of any discussion of taxation and politics: Is taxation better politics than the alternatives—expanded money supply, inactive government, or more foreign aid?

My answer is "yes." The reasons for this answer have in most instances been at least partially developed previously. These reasons are:

1. Finance of expenditures through an expanded money supply removes the most important brake on excessive and extravagant government expenditures, which will later certainly result in political scandals and ousting of the government. This brake is needed particularly in underdeveloped countries where the countervail-

ing forces to government expenditure schemes are particularly weak.

2. The use of more foreign aid is certain to strengthen the cry of "foreign lacky" and will lead to the development of other groups who can bear the banner of nationalism higher than can the government. This is politically very dangerous in areas where nationalism, because of the proud possession of a recently won independence, is extremely strong.

3. A government that does not undertake new projects becomes a "do-nothing government" and the vigorous and forward-looking elements of the country look to other groups to carry their plans into reality.

4. An inactive government soon becomes a government that, to the people, appears to be a government without purpose or merit. Therefore, the voters lose interest in government as a means of improving their welfare.

5. Inflation is very *likely* (in a country such as Viet-Nam, the writer believes *always* is the better word) to follow expenditures out of an expanded money supply. Inflation in an area such as Viet-Nam tends to increase the gap between the rich and the poor, which development provides a fertile breeding ground for an expansion of communism.

6. If funds that are spent come from abroad and/or from an expanded money supply, controls over corruption are weakened, and numerous and serious examples of corruption are certain to develop.

7. The citizens of a new nation are prepared to make sacrifices to speed up development. This is a portion of the appeal of communism. If a government does not provide this opportunity, it strengthens the opposition and its support of the Spartan life.

8. A good tax system partially corrects many economic injustices arising out of favoritism, chance, and the operations of the market place. Without this correction, the government will be subjected to additional abuse, and ammunition will be furnished to rival groups.

9. Unsavory elements of the population rise to high positions under conditions of inflation (expanded

money supply) and foreign assistance. These groups will become closely associated with the government and will lead to a general loss of respect for the government.

10. A government financing its means with taxes becomes a moral government and will increase the morality of the electorate. This is the politically sound course in any country and, particularly, in a nation that has just experienced the immorality of colonial rule and war.

This list of ten is not meant to exhaust the points I have previously mentioned and, of course, not to exhaust the subject. The list is merely meant to be illustrative of some of the relatively short-run politically favorable elements of a sound tax program. In the long run the political arguments for a wide expansion of tax collections seem to be unquestionably stronger than the short-run points.

Desirability of an Expenditure Tax

*The following analysis appeared in the 5 March 1953
issue of Economics and Commerce, published at the University of Panjab in Pakistan.*

*Professor Lindholm is protesting the desirability of
an expenditure tax being initiated in Pakistan, as recommended by Mr. Colin Clark. Again, the analysis has
general applicability: All too often emerging nations
are advised to adopt economic measures that are difficult to administer and are basically untried.*

Mr. Colin Clark in his economic report based on a Colombo-financed
analysis of Pakistan presents a forthright and well-integrated set of
recommendations. The points made by this distinguished economist
have great value as presented. However, Pakistan can gain even more
if the pivotal points of Mr. Clark's economic report are the subject of
further scrutiny. This first discussion will examine only the portion of
the recommendations related to the revision of the Pakistan income tax.

Mr. Clark in his taxation recommendation proposes "to exclude
from taxable income the entire amount saved out of that income
during the year." This broad exclusion of savings is later modified
by the definition of taxable income as net income the past year, less
the amounts spent in the purchase or construction of assets in Pakistan, plus receipts from the sale or liquidation of assets, less the net
increase of liabilities in Pakistan, and less income tax paid during the
previous year.

The principal effect of this provision is to limit savings for the
purposes of reducing tax liability to net investment made in Pakistan.
Deductible savings are further limited by listing the types of assets,
the acquisition or construction of which are not an acceptable use of
savings. In Mr. Clark's words, "assets for the above purpose should not
include coin, notes, gold, jewelry, furniture, motor cars, works of art
and such personal possessions, or agricultural land." The assets considered acceptable are also defined but the classification is more general than that of excluded assets. "They should, in general, include all

classes of property used for business, all classes of real property and
bank deposits. They should include all shares in companies or partnerships provided it can be shown that such companies or partnerships
are formed solely for business purposes and are not a disguised form
of personal expenditure."

Fundamentally Mr. Clark has proposed to substitute a spendings
tax for the income tax, with taxable spendings limited to those uses
of income and liquidated assets that might be generally defined as
purchase of consumer goods and investment outside of Pakistan plus
investment in agricultural land. Taxation proposals of this type are
not unusual and have been rather common when schemes to increase savings and investment were under consideration. During
World War II an expenditure tax in addition to the income tax gained
considerable support in all the nations of the world. Also, labor groups
of the United States, particularly the CIO, advocated the use of a
spendings tax rather than an increase of the personal income tax to
meet the additional revenue requirements of the U.S. Government
after the outbreak of the Korean War in 1950. Because of the different conditions in the United States, the spendings taxes recommended have not excluded additional assets acquired abroad or the
purchase of agricultural land from the definition of savings.

The taxation of spendings rather than income is recommended
when additional savings to finance investment are needed to advance
the general welfare. The tax also gains popular support when it
seems likely a sales tax will be introduced. The spendings tax is advanced as a tax which will reduce consumer spending as efficiently
as the sales tax, bring in the additional revenue expected from the
sales tax, and in addition prove to be more just.

The advantages of the spendings tax are so substantial that they
make one wonder why the tax has not been generally adopted. The
tax's weaknesses that have caused it not to be adopted are largely
administrative. These administrative difficulties are sufficiently great
to warrant serious consideration and should not be brushed aside by
the statement—"This method will involve considerable administrative changes, and also increased work for business accountants; but
the cost involved should be very small compared with the contributions to the national economy which will result"—as Mr. Clark has
done.

Some aspects of the seriousness of these administrative problems
can be made clear through a number of simple illustrations.

In the first place, the introduction of the spendings tax requires
that every taxpayer submit a complete accounting of his assets; otherwise the amount of new investments cannot be ascertained. The value
of these assets under even the most favorable conditions of a personal

audit and evaluation by both an economist and an investment expert would be difficult. In addition, court cases challenging the accuracy of the valuation would continue for years. This type of careful audit would be impractical even in a highly developed country and would be impossible in Pakistan. Without this careful evaluation each taxpayer's word as to the value of his assets would have to be accepted.

The well-advised taxpayer upon the introduction of this system would greatly overvalue his assets. In fact, Mr. Clark in his innocence recommends that high asset values should be encouraged by granting a general amnesty to all taxpayers who have accumulated assets through avoidance or evasion of the present income tax. Overvaluation becomes to the interest of the taxpayer because, as Mr. Clark says, "under this system (expenditure tax), we should assess with income all capital gains, so far as they are spent, and *give credit for capital losses.*" The italicized portion of recommendation, which is almost a necessary portion of legislation establishing an expenditure tax, provides the basic reason for the desirability of overvaluing assets. If an asset is valued at Rs. 10 *lakhs* and is sold for Rs. 5 *lakhs,* the taxpayer suffered a capital loss of 5 *lakhs.* The expenditure of the taxpayer for the year may be only Rs. 5 *lakhs*; and, of course, under these conditions he would not pay any expenditure tax.

This procedure of avoiding an expenditure tax is obviously more available to an owner of property than to a worker on a salary. The weakness cited above is important; but it can be argued that, as time passes and these overvalued assets are sold, the importance of the loophole will disappear. This philosophical attitude may be commendable, but the avoidance of taxes in this fashion could develop strong political pressures. However, as can be illustrated, it is very nearly necessary to use the unrealized concept of capital gains and losses rather than realized. Under these conditions capital assets need not be sold to benefit from capital losses, as will be shown in the following discussion.

The balance sheet of a taxpayer is assumed to be as given below on 1 January 1952, and it is also assumed to be exactly the same

TAXPAYER'S BALANCE SHEET

Assets		Liabilities	
	Rs.		Rs.
Cash	100,000	Bank loan	100,000
Stocks and bonds	200,000	Mortgage	20,000
(1953 plus 60,000)			
Residence	40,000	Total liability	120,000
		Total worth	220,000
Total assets	340,000		

on 1 January 1953 with the exception that the stocks and bonds amount goes up to 260,000.

During 1953 the total income of the taxpayer including salary, dividends, and interest from assets held is Rs. 180,000. During the year the taxpayer purchases Rs. 60,000 of additional stocks and bonds and also sells Rs. 60,000 of stocks and bonds. An expenditure tax is levied on the amount spent for consumption during the year and the amount invested is not to be taxed. Deducting new investment from income leaves Rs. 120,000 that the taxpayer must have spent for consumption purposes, but the taxpayer actually spent Rs. 60,000 in addition to the Rs. 120,000. This, however, does not make its appearance in the balance sheet because it is further assumed that during the year the market value of the stocks and bonds account increased by the Rs. 60,000 realized by the sale of stocks and bonds.

If only realized capital gains are to be considered income, as Mr. Clark recommends, then only a portion of the Rs. 60,000 received by the taxpayer through the sale of securities are capital gains. If in the example given it is assumed that all stocks and bonds increased by an equal percentage, then only Rs. 20,000 (30 per cent) would be capital gains and would be considered income from which investment would be deducted in calculating the expenditure tax. The effect is to increase taxable expenditure (consumption expenditure) to Rs. 140,000. However, this is still Rs. 40,000 less than was actually spent. There is no way of taxing the additional Rs. 40,000 of expenditures under an expenditure tax unless unrealized capital gains are withheld from the taxpayer's balance sheet or unless unrealized capital gains are considered income. Both of these possible solutions create great additional difficulties.

If it is decided to tax unrealized capital gains, then unrealized capital losses must also be deducted. This solution opens the door to the writing down of assets without sale and provides a loophole that would greatly reduce tax collections from those best able to pay. If instead the solution of not including capital gains in the balance sheet is adopted, it becomes impossible to utilize the change of assets of the taxpayer in calculating expenditures, and reliance must be placed on expenditure data. This latter solution has as many outrageous developments as the utilization of unrealized capital gains and losses.

The expenditure tax advocated by Mr. Clark has many features that recommend it when the examination remains on the level of general principles. However, when the tax is examined in the light of administration problems, it is seen to be badly suited for use in an underdeveloped country. The aim of increasing investment will not only be missed, but in introducing the tax, the fiscal agencies of the government are likely to become bogged down. The apparent injustice added to the reduction of revenues may seriously undermine the entire economy. Mr. Clark's intentions are no doubt the best; however, following his tax advice would not only fail to advance the aims of the Colombo plan but would seriously retard them in Pakistan.

Part III

LAND REFORM
IN SOUTH VIET-NAM

Economic Implications
of the Agrarian
Reform Ordinance

*The following selection was given as a lecture by Pro-
fessor Lindholm at the National Institute of Administration in Saigon.*

*He gives a section by section analysis of the basic
land reform legislation. The findings point to difficulties inherent in the program. Many of these difficulties
and others have developed since 1957 when the analysis
was written.*

On 22 October 1956 Ordinance No. 57 was issued by the government of Viet-Nam.[1] The purpose of this Ordinance is to establish the
way in which the large private land holdings of Viet-Nam are to be
divided into small privately owned holdings.

Article 3 of the Ordinance sets the maximum land holdings[2] at 100
hectares, only 30 of which may actually be exploited by the landowner. This seems to mean that a landlord may not operate a rice
farm in excess of 30 hectares. In this provision is the economic assumption that it is more important for the size of ownership of rice
land to remain relatively large (200 hectares) than for the size of
cultivation to remain large (30 hectares). The apparent basis of this
position is that it is more vital that the landlord's income based on
rents remain sufficient to provide a certain level of income than that
the cultivation of rice on a rather large scale under one ownership be
possible.

It may be that in order for Viet-Nam to raise the per capita income and still compete on the international rice markets, it will be

---

[1] This Ordinance was published in the *Official Gazette of the Republic of Viet-
Nam,* 29 October 1956.

[2] It is implied that the maximum relates only to rice land; but Article 4 excludes land used to raise industrial crops, which appears to include land used to
raise any crop other than rice.

necessary to use modern rice cultivation methods. Under the law, modern rice cultivation methods are possible only if landlords can use the required equipment cooperatively. It seems that large-scale production might be more important in bringing about efficient production procedures in the cultivation of rice than would be the case in the cultivation of coffee, fruit, tobacco, and a number of other crops where the size of cultivation is *not* limited. Because of this, it might not be desirable to limit the sacrifice involved in the land reform legislation to owners of rice land. This aim could be met along the lines of additional national tax on agricultural land other than rice land, which would have a rate that would increase with the size of the holding.

Article 7, which is largely an administrative article, may also have considerable economic importance. It states that "Parcels recorded in the real estate register in the name of the same owner are considered as a single personal property." This Article does not mention whether separate treatment will be given to properties listed in the names of different persons of the same family. With the family organization continuing strong in Viet-Nam and the family control existing over a rather large number of persons, this provision would certainly permit the continuation of family holdings of very extensive properties. India, to avoid a somewhat similar problem in the collection of income taxes with progressive rates, has based the rates applicable on the income of the undivided Hindu family. The undivided family is treated largely as though it were a single individual or a single association or business firm.

Articles 9 and 10, by declaring any transfer of ownership rights made after the decree null and void and declaring that estates should be considered as undivided, attempt to avoid the problem of not treating property ownership on a family basis but rather on an individual basis. In doing this, certain undesirable restrictions are created particularly in the regular purchase and sale of property arising out of normal business operations. This problem of separate ownership but group control is, of course, a major difficulty inherent in all efforts to determine size of property by legal means. In the areas of the world where ownership of large properties has proven to be a hindrance to a rising per capita income and to the development of democratic institutions, the taxes collected on large properties under joint or single control have been inadequate. In addition, the taxes levied on estates at death have been inadequate.

The economic advantage of using the taxation procedure rather than legal restriction of size is that it 1) provides additional revenues for the government rather than reducing revenues and increasing expenditures, as is likely to be the case when legislation requiring property division is utilized; and 2) permits a particularly efficient land-user to keep his land by meeting the high government tax requirements. Both of these effects provide conditions under which per capita income is likely to be stimulated more than through the legal division of property. Article 14 provides that the property acquired through the redistribution of land be paid in six years, but the payment is not to include the 3 per cent interest paid to the former owners. This payment period is very short. When these large annual payment requirements are related to Article 30, which apparently provides for immediate government repossession in case of payment default, we have the establishment of conditions which a new operator is likely to find very difficult to meet.

Although the Ordinance does not provide that the land taxes must be paid by the new recipient, this seems to be assumed in the last portion of Article 11. Also, because title to the land remains with the government, the new user of the land does not have an opportunity to borrow on the basis of his equity in the land. Article 16 further provides that the land may not be mortgaged for an additional four-year period, making a total of ten years when the principal asset of the cultivator may not be used as security to finance working capital improvements or for the purchase of additional land to make his holdings more economical.

The reasons behind these provisions are understandable and the motives cannot be impugned. Certainly the difficulties they were attempting to guard against have in the past been very real. But it is also true that these restrictions make it more difficult for a new cultivator 1) to borrow to meet a payment in a year when he might have a crop failure or to meet unusual financial demands or 2) to purchase new equipment and expand his holdings if he proves to be an efficient farmer. The repossession provision is very vigorous (Article 30) and the payments, if to cover only a six-year period, must be high.

It would seem that some provision to borrow on the basis of equity in the land would be necessary to prevent uneconomical operations arising from discouragement and short-term planning based on Article 14, which provides that "The first installment must be paid after the harvest of the year following the year in which he took possession of the land." Also, restrictions which prevent the efficient farmers from utilizing their assets as a basis of loans to finance expansion and improvement of production activities is undesirable in a country such as Viet-Nam, which is striving to increase its per capita income. It is a rather well-established principle in economic development that short-term operations not providing for the maintenance and improvement of production capacity should be discouraged and the efficient operators should be encouraged to expand. The Ordinance may violate this principle.

The most interesting aspect of this Ordinance is covered in Articles 21 and 22. These two articles provide the method of payment to the owners of the rice land that is to be redistributed. The payment is to be made by the government at the time the land is made available to it for later distribution among the eligible recipients in the order of the priority established in Article 12. Ten per cent of the total payment is made in cash and the remainder "by registered nontransferable bonds guaranteed by the state bearing an annual interest of 3 per cent and amortized in 12 years." Although these bonds are generally nonnegotiable, they may be used to pay "land and inheritance taxes owned on the expropriated lands." In addition, they may be used at par value to pay for a "subscription to securities of any enterprises created by the state in the framework of a program of national economic development."

Article 32 makes provision for the funds to pay the 10 per cent cash payment. This Article fails to set down the source of the funds to be used, but it does provide for the establishment of an autonomous fund and an audit system which is to be determined by a later decree.

Before analyzing what these provisions *do* accomplish, I will consider briefly some things that are *not done*. The Ordinance makes no provision for raising the amount that would be required to make the 10 per cent payment. Since the budget of the national government is more likely in the foreseeable future to run a deficit than a surplus, it appears that these funds could only be made available by a grant from some foreign country. This would generate the required counterpart piasters for government use to accomplish the provisions of the Ordinance. Or the funds may arise from the expansion of government borrowing from citizen savers or from new money created by the National Bank under the powers provided it in Ordinance No. 48.

I haven't heard a carefully calculated figure as to the quantity of land that would be redistributed, but a modest program would redistribute about 700,000 hectares (100,000 families with an average size farm of 7 hectares) at an average price of 15,000 piasters per hectare. This would make the total value of redistributed land equal to about 10.5 billion piasters—on this basis, a cash payment of slightly over one billion piasters or about 30 million dollars at the official rate of exchange at which American aid has been given. If the slightly over one billion piasters were made available through expansion of the credit of the National Bank, it would bring about a direct expansion of the money supply of Viet-Nam by over 6 per cent and provide reserves for a further expansion of demand deposits of four to five times more, for a possible total expansion of the money supply by 25 per cent. If the funds were to be raised by new taxes, it would require an increase of tax collections for one year by about 20 per cent. It is doubtful that bonds could be sold to voluntary savers unless the interest offered were nearly 10 per cent or the value of the piaster had been stabilized for quite some period. The last of these alternatives is certainly not available if immediate action is desired, and the high interest rate would more than likely be difficult to put into effect when those having their land redistributed receive only 3 per cent on the bonds. In addition, the 3 per cent interest on approximately 9 billion piasters of bonds outstanding would require an annual payment from regular Treasury revenues of 270 million piasters, because Article 14 does not provide for payment of interest to the government by the new landowners.

A person is justified in concluding that the program as envisaged will on its initiation set in motion considerable inflationary pressures, expansion of foreign aid, or a very substantial expansion of the tax burden. We have seen that the tax collection agencies of Viet-Nam have not as yet modernized their operations to the extent necessary to permit collection of additional taxes. This leaves us with the alternatives of the creation of inflationary pressures or the receipt of additional foreign aid. Either of these alternatives has its undesirable qualities, unless the foreign aid can be increased. If it is only used for land reform, it means that some 30 million dollars are used to finance the original cash payment for the land redistribution program that could have been used to build a sugar refinery or a textile factory that would have reduced Viet-Nam's need for imports and increased the productivity of Vietnamese labor. However, this possible benefit must be weighed against the benefit to be expected from the redistribution of land, which will give many Vietnamese the chance of becoming small landowners. If the money supply is expanded, the resulting increase in prices will lead to numerous unfavorable results.

Although these economic aspects of the program as set down in Articles 21 and 22 are important, they are perhaps outweighed by the provision that the bonds received by the landlord can be used in payment for subscriptions in "enterprises created by the state in the framework of a program of national economic development." The obvious economic purpose of this provision is to give landlords who are losing land an opportunity to become industrialists. The purpose can certainly be lauded but its implementation may cause economic difficulties.

For example, when the former landlord gives his bonds to the treasurer of a new Vietnamese business enterprise, he will receive in exchange securities indicating ownership in the enterprise. The bonds received by the treasurer only represent earnings of 3 per cent on the face value plus the gradual repayment of the bonds by the government during the 12-year period as established in Article 21. This gradual repayment will provide the enterprise with cash during this period, which will more than likely be useful and might permit it to pay dividends on its operations when otherwise this would be impossible because all the earnings would be needed to meet development expenditures. However, the real need of the new business will be spendable funds available to meet the costs of originally getting under way, and this need cannot be met by the landlord's bonds—at least not directly. Also, it is doubtful that the landlord would be willing to make his bonds available to a new business for their use and in return to receive only a 3 per cent rate of interest. However, if the return were more than this and the bonds were only held as a means of assuring a certain amount of annual cash income, it would be necessary for the business to pay this additional return out of capital, for the mere holding of the bonds of the landlord would not provide the additional funds that would be needed.

This very cursory analysis of the usefulness and the problems related to the use of landlord bonds to meet the financing needs of a new business makes very evident that they would not meet important financing needs, unless they could either be used as collateral for a loan from the commercial banks of Viet-Nam, the National Bank, or some other credit agency. Article 22 does not mention the way landlord bonds can be used after receipt by the new business, but neither does it say that they cannot be purchased or discounted by the National Bank. However, the provision that title is nontransferable would seriously restrict the use of these bonds as collateral.

A way out of this difficulty may be provided in the first sentence of Article 22, which states "The aforesaid bonds may be pledged and are legal tender for mortgage debts contracted with the Agricultural Credit Agency." If this route were selected, the procedure would be something like this: A landlord could put up the property still in his possession as security for a mortgage loan, and after the loan was received he could use his bonds to retire the mortgage. This would leave him with free funds to assist in the financing of an industrial enterprise while the land still owned would again be free; and if later additional funds were needed to develop these lands, the landlord could apply for a mortgage loan. This procedure would permit monetizing landlord bonds within the provisions of Ordinance No. 57, but in doing this it raises a number of other questions: Where will the Agricultural Credit Agency obtain its funds? Why under these circumstances would the landlord place his new liquid assets into a new industry? Why wouldn't he purchase gold instead?

I shall not discuss any more ramifications of Ordinance No. 57. However, I do still have a number of questions. I hope I will be pardoned if I merely mention these without attempting an answer; actually some of these questions cannot be answered without additional information, but some are inherent in the provisions of the Ordinance.

Will it be possible for the Agricultural Credit Agency to sell the landlord bonds it receives to the National Bank of Viet-Nam or to the commercial banks of Viet-Nam in order to permit it to continue its lending operation? Can the new business developed under the national economic development program use the landlord bonds they received to obtain working capital? Can the landlord bonds issued be cashed at the death of the original holder to settle the estate? Is the repayment of a 100 per cent agricultural land contract within 6 years too brief a period? Why will the government continue to make payments of interest on the landlord bonds beyond the period of receipt of the face value of the bonds from the new landlord? What are the rules under which the committees operate that set the value of land and buildings? Why should only the land on which rice is raised be subject to land reform? If the land is idle can it be considered to be land unsuitable to the cultivation of rice? After land suitable for rice has been switched to another culture, can title to the land be divided among members of the family and then later can the land be returned to rice culture; and in this way the requirements of land reform avoided? Does the Ordinance have a time limit or does it continue into perpetuity? How can the landlords protect themselves against a falling value of the piaster? Can the landlord bonds be used in some fashion to meet the monetary requirements arising out of an emergency?

These are rather specific questions. There are other economic questions of a more general nature which might be asked. Some of these which come to mind are: Will the Ordinance increase the ability of Viet-Nam to compete on the world rice markets? Is it desirable that land other than rice be held in tracts of unlimited size? Will the ownership pattern of rice lands be determined by economic factors with legal decrees having at the most only a temporary effect? Will economic pressures cause landlord bonds, originally issued under strict nonnegotiable requirements, to be changed later to permit them to be used as the basis for a considerable credit expansion?

An Economic Development-Oriented Land Reform Program for Viet-Nam

This article is reprinted with permission from the book "Land Tenure, Industrialization and Social Stability," Walter Froelich, ed., published in 1961 by the Marquette University Press in Milwaukee.

The economic potential of Viet-Nam's agriculture is assessed in the light of the agricultural programs being followed by the government. The programs are found to be inadequate because they assume that the countryside has a lower standard of living than the city, and that agriculture can continue to be carried out by the use of traditional agricultural production methods.

A comment on Professor Lindholm's proposals by Nguyen Phu Duc follows the article.

This paper is divided into three parts. The first part summarizes the agricultural situation in Viet-nam and the historical conditions which caused the development. The second deals with those forces at work in Viet-Nam which seem to require a new approach to agriculture. The third part presents an agricultural program to meet the long-term industrial development and social stability needs of Viet-Nam.

I.

Rice remains the principal agricultural crop of Viet-Nam and the principal product produced. The Vietnamese farmer whose main crop is not rice continues to be the exception.

Rice was being cultivated by people living along the Red River (North Viet-Nam) in 1,000 B.C.[1] The Vietnamese civilization as developed in its present location has always been a rice civilization. It

---

[1] Joseph Bittinger, *The Smaller Dragon* (New York: Frederick A. Praeger, 1958), p. 68.

is estimated that 75 per cent of the population work directly on the land or are completely dependent on the efforts of others who do. This gives Viet-Nam an agricultural population of about nine million. These nine million persons produced an income, according to the most recent estimate of Viet-Nam's national income, of 27.4 billion piasters. This means that about 75 per cent of the population of Viet-Nam, making a living from agriculture, produced only about 24 per cent of the income of the country. This average income per capita is about 3,000 piasters, or somewhere between 50 and 70 U.S. dollars.[2]

It is true throughout the world that the income of the rural people tends to be less than that enjoyed by the city dwellers. A part of this difference certainly arises from the difference in prices prevailing for similar goods and services in the country and in the city. Another portion of the difference is accounted for by the inherent difficulty in determining the quantity of home produced and consumed food, shelter, and clothing used by people living on the farm. Finally, a large portion of the income of persons in the city is used in going to and from the job and meeting other requirements of earning the income enjoyed. These expenditures are included in income, but in reality they constitute a part of the income production cost and are not a base for a higher level of enjoyable consumption. To the extent that this relationship exists, the incomes (living standards) of the people living in the cities are overestimated. Also, in thinking of incomes of people living in the tropics, it must be realized that these people do not require an income to purchase heavy clothing or fuel to keep them warm in winter nor do they require houses built to withstand winter weather. These additional protective expenditures absorb 10 to 15 per cent of the income of persons inhabiting temperate climate areas.[3]

Viet-Nam is not a rich country but neither is it a poor country. The person living in the city has an average per capita gross income of about 12,000 piasters. This is a purchasing power of about $500 and would give the average Vietnamese city family of six a gross income of $3,000. These estimates indicate that a family in Saigon can afford a small automobile and is able to provide for the education of the children. However, this standard of living is at the average only available to about 25 per cent of the population.

In utilizing national income data one must remember the low degree of reliability. The margin of error is actually very wide. This situation exists partially because of inadequate statistics. A more funda-

---

[2] This is also the approximate rural income level in the middle income countries of Latin America. Wendell C. Gordon, *The Economy of Latin America* (New York: Columbia University Press, 1950), p. 355.

[3] Carl S. Shoup, *Principles of National Income Analysis* (New York: Houghton Mifflin, 1947), p. 13.

mental explanation, however, is that the basic concepts of the national income and product amounts are based on the assumption of a
market economy something like that existing in Western Europe or
the United States.[4] When these concepts are applied to a people still
living mostly in a traditional village rice culture, they fit very badly.
Here I can speak with some authority as I was largely responsible for
initiating the national income and product estimates for Viet-Nam.[5]
However, despite the shortcomings of these data, they provide the
best picture of the existing economic situation that is suitable for study,
evaluation, and comparison.

Although agriculture can be said to be Viet-Nam's most important industry, the gross domestic product by sector of origin shows
that commerce is just as important. These two sectors combined accounted for 48 per cent of the total value of product produced in 1955.

Using these same incomplete and inadequate national income and
product data of Viet-Nam, we find that some seven billion piasters of
the income of the rural population arose from the cultivation of rice.
This is about 40 per cent of the total value of agricultural and live-
stock product produced in Viet-Nam and about 25 per cent of the total
product allocated to the 75 per cent of Viet-Nam's population classified as rural.[6]

Although rice is the principal crop of Viet-Nam and the conditions
of Viet-Nam seem to be ideally suited to rice cultivation, the rice
produced in Viet-Nam has not been able to effectively meet world
competition in the period following World War II.[7] A study of rice
productivity per hectare of land shows that Japan produces some 34.3
quintals per hectare of paddy while Viet-Nam produces only 13.0. This
places Viet-Nam very near the bottom. The reasons are many, but certainly an important cause is the failure of Vietnamese farmers to invest as much time and money in the growing of their rice crops as
do the Japanese or Korean farmers. They do not select their seed as
carefully; they have not been on the lookout for improved seeds; they
do not plant their fields as carefully; they do not fertilize as completely;
and they are more careless in harvesting and protecting their crops.
The Vietnamese farmer has not been as efficient as his counterpart in
Japan.

---

[4] Central Statistical Office (Great Britain), *National Income Statistics, Sources and Methods* (London: Her Majesty's Stationery Office, 1956), p. 37.

[5] USOM/Saigon, *Estimates of National Income Accounts for Viet-Nam*
(1954).

[6] R. W. Lindholm, ed., *Viet-Nam: The First Five Years* (East Lansing:
Michigan State University Press, 1959), p. 180.

[7] The rice being exported from the 1959 crop is receiving nearly a 50 per cent
subsidy. A country such as Viet-Nam cannot follow this type of program on a
permanent basis.

Secondary food crops and commercial agricultural products of Viet-Nam have been generally gaining in importance. By far the most important of these developments was the introduction of rubber cultivation into Viet-Nam in 1897 by Raoul, a French Navy pharmacist who sent 2,000 plants of *hevea brasiliensis* from Malaya to be planted in the Saigon Botanical Garden.[8] The first successful rubber plantation operator was Beland, chief of detectives in Saigon, who tapped his trees for the first time in 1905. The cultivation of rubber trees has remained largely a plantation operation, owned by French-dominated companies and managed by French plantation operators. Recently the Vietnamese have shown more interest in the activity. It is rather surprising that the interest of the Vietnamese has not been greater.

Coffee and tea cultivation are appropriate to the climate and soil of parts of Viet-Nam, particularly to the red soils of the highlands. Here again the French colonists took the lead in the development, and again the Vietnamese have only very recently shown an interest in the activity. Secondary food crops, that is food other than rice, have been grown for quite some time, with some American plants introduced by the Chinese as early as the 16th century. The secondary food crops include corn, sweet potatoes, beans, manioc, and taro. These crops are excellent providers of nutrients required for a balanced diet. Sweet potatoes, as one case in point, serve to meet basic diet requirements more economically than does rice.

In addition to these vegetables, fruits such as bananas and papayas provide an important portion of the diet of the people. Also, the coconut tree has been developed, and kapok continues to find favor. This partial listing of agricultural products shows that Viet-Nam possesses conditions suitable for the development of a varied agriculture. It also possesses rich fishing grounds, and dried fish is an old product of Viet-Nam.[9]

These secondary crops, unless developed along plantation lines by the French, have been used largely to supplement the basic diet of rice and fish sauce *(nuc-mom)* of the Vietnamese farmer. Their cultivation has not been carried out seriously as a commercial enterprise. The planting, harvesting, and cultivation has been carried out in a haphazard fashion.

Vietnamese agricultural practices and land use, and the attitude of the government of Viet-Nam toward land reform and land taxation, are best understood after a brief summary of the development of Vietnamese village practices. The Vietnamese colonized and thus gained

---

[8] Lindholm, *op. cit.*, p. 192.

[9] Charles Robequain, *The Economic Development of French Indo-China* (London: Oxford University Press, 1944), pp. 225-41.

control of the area now included in Viet-Nam (South) relatively recently. At the time of the arrival of the French during the middle of
the 19th century, the Vietnamese were still in the process of occupy-
ing the rich farm lands along the Mekong.[10] In order to consolidate
these new areas either unsettled or inhabited by the Chams or Cam-
bodians, the Vietnamese rulers created military colonies to settle
villages along the newly established frontiers and made large land
grants to ranking mandarins in recognition of their services. To develop his new estate, the mandarin would recruit settlers—mostly
from the mandarin's own native village—and advance the peasants
money to clear land and establish intensive rice culture. Any moun-
tainous land that happened to fall within the military conquest was
allowed to remain as it was with no attempt at development. These
new settlers were given some of the land cleared as private holdings,
and the mandarin retained the balance of the area, collecting rent
from it and imposing taxes on the village as a whole. However, the
mandarin did not mix in the internal affairs of the village, which were
administered by the villagers themselves. When the mandarin died his
land was supposed to revert to the village as communal land, and
many times this was the case, particularly around the city of Hue.[11]
This reverting of land to the village was less likely to take place in
the areas along the Mekong.

The settlements of the Vietnamese along the Mekong were greatly
expanded by the work of the French. The French built long canals that
opened large tracts that had been previously inaccessible to the Vietnamese. By encouraging settlement through improved drainage and
facilitating transport and communications, the canals, dug largely at
the expense of the colonial government, were the decisive factor in
the development of the area into the rice bowl of Viet-Nam. Some of
these new lands were owned by the French, but frequently the ownership was vested in the Vietnamese, who cultivated the land through
tenants working small four- to six-acre plots. Under these conditions
the old concept of the village as the originating center for land-use
policies largely disappeared. Unfortunately the Vietnamese landowner
did not take advantage of the opportunity by increasing his interest
in the technology of agriculture. His son studied law rather than
agronomy when he went to school in France.

An extended postwar period of lawlessness made the old type of
Vietnamese land use and control through the village appear attractive, and many of the isolated farmers clustered together in villages and
ceased paying rent to the landowner. Again land began to be regarded

---

10 Bittinger, *op. cit.*, p. 350.
11 Raleigh Barlowe, *Land Resource Economics* (Englewood Cliffs: Prentice-
Hall, 1958), pp. 330-31.

as the communal property of the village, and old Vietnamese customs were cited to take the land out of private ownership and make it the common property of the village. The religious sects which developed at this time, the Cao Dai being the largest, appealed to this heritage and found a ready response among the peasants. With the re-establishment of order in Viet-Nam the government became interested in having the thousands of acres of abandoned land brought under cultivation. These were lands that had not been cultivated under the village organization re-established during the period of turmoil. The policies established to expand cultivation showed the influence of the old Vietnamese idea of communal land, and peasants willingly worked land without having title to it. They did not fear that someone on the basis of a formal land record would take their land from them. To do this would be completely out of context with their culture.[12]

The current government efforts to increase the utilization of the upland regions have again been centered around the Vietnamese traditional land-use pattern. Some 36 sites to include 50,000 families are being developed within the Vietnamese tradition of individually owned holdings plus communal land available to those farmers wishing to use it and willing to pay the established rent. Under the tradition the rent from these communal lands provides the village with the revenues required to meet its outlays.

Turning now from the land-use pattern to the technology employed, we find that the methods utilized in raising and harvesting rice in Viet-Nam are the traditional methods developed in Asia two thousand years ago. The farmers have not been able to organize a procedure for utilizing the better strains of rice as seed despite strenuous efforts initiated in the 1930's by the Indo-China Rice Service, a public, incorporated institution.[13] Very few of the large owners of rice land have introduced mechanical equipment but instead are content to continue to cultivate in the old way. The efforts of American experts and Western-trained Vietnamese to introduce improved agricultural methods have been only moderately successful during the past five years.

It is because the agricultural tools and methods are very inefficient that agriculture requires such a large portion of the Vietnamese population. And it is this large portion of the population engaged in agriculture that arises to concern anybody who seriously considers modernizing agriculture. For modernization would at the very least reduce by half the number of persons needed to tend the land, and in many cases would increase many times the amount of land cultivated by one

---

[12] The impact of domestic cultural and political forces and how they affect programs is discussed in W. W. Rostow, *The Process of Economic Growth* (New York: W. W. Norton, 1952), pp. 224-25.

[13] Robequain, *op. cit.,* p. 229.

individual. Basically, of course, modern cultivation requires that the size of the area cultivated by one entrepreneur be of a size suitable to a combination of the factors of production that can produce a low-cost product and give a high level of income to the operator.

II.

There are a number of forces at work in Viet-Nam which will inevitably bring about major changes in the agriculture of Viet-Nam and in the distribution and size of the population of Viet-Nam. Before introducing the qualifications necessary for our analysis, consideration of the size of the gross impact of the population is in order.

The birth rate of Viet-Nam is not definitely known, but the better estimates indicate that it is approximately 30 per 1,000 inhabitants per year. This rate would double the population in 23 years and quadruple it in 46 years. This would bring the population up to about 28 million in 1982 and to 48 million in 2005. If the population in the Saigon-Cholon area would be only proportional to the increase in the rest of the country, its population would increase to the present size of New York City. The trends evident in other countries point to an even more rapid growth of Saigon-Cholon as a metropolitan area.

This tendency toward rapid expansion of established large cities in countries at the threshold of development is of sufficient interest to warrant a more complete consideration than can be given here. That matter has been developed elsewhere in the literature of economic development. The tendency for a few large cities to become ever larger and to grow at the expense, as it were, of the rest of the nation is evident in Southeast Asia, in parts of Africa, and certainly in Latin America. One writer in the area of urban development in speaking of the cities of the South American nations says, "Today, this tendency toward unbalanced urbanization patterns, by which the population concentrates in a single big city in each country or major region, continues to strengthen itself with enormous population increases in most countries."[14]

The growth of these cities makes clear a number of very important influences which the leaders of these countries have not had a sufficient opportunity to explore. The fundamental cause of this very widespread influx of rural populations into the capital city seems to have its roots in a deep feeling that the life on the land is no longer meaningful and that the city somehow symbolizes the new possibilities open to all people now that the secrets of the West are known. Such other factors as disorder in the countryside have been important, but they are not

[14] From an unpublished manuscript by Professor Francis Vilich, Chairman, Department of City and Regional Planning, University of California (Berkeley), titled "Urban Land Use in South America," p. 2.

fundamental; rather, they represent results of the fundamental cause. The man working on the land with primitive tools becomes discouraged, dissatisfied, and morose when he hears on the radio or sees in the movies how what he is doing can be done and is being done in many parts of the world. And when he also sees and hears how people who till the soil live elsewhere, he wishes to emulate them. The only possibility of doing this that seems to be remotely realizable is to move to his country's population center.

The plea of the peasant for land today consists of the mouthings of political leaders and others who have not kept up with the rush of events. It is the cry of the 19th century and not of the mid-20th century and will certainly be forgotten before the end of the 20th century. The current cry, which can be heard from the steppes of Russia to the rice paddies of Japan, a cry that will be a part of the thinking of Vietnamese before many years, is for modern equipment, modern methods, and first-rate raw materials. In the case of agriculture the cry is for an institutional framework which permits the size of the agricultural operating unit to be readily determined by the size required for lowest cost operation.

If this approach gets somewhat closer to the fundamental forces at work in agriculture than does the repetition of old slogans, then Viet-Nam's land reform program may be a lot of to-do about nothing.[15] Today a man cannot be happy living as his ancestors did, nor can he obtain the satisfaction tradition says he should from running the soil through his fingers—his soil and his land. This, however, is not evidenced by an examination of the so-called revolutionary programs of land use and development being pushed by many developing countries. Rather than looking forward, they seem to be holding time back and using the old slogans long after they have lost their true ring.

The population level of Viet-Nam will have outrun the productivity of traditional agriculture within a very few years, as modern medicine becomes generally available. Even if food could be provided in sufficient quantity through improved fertilizers and seeds and better sowing and reaping methods applied to the old techniques, there remains the basic question: Why should such a large portion of the population spend their lives producing the the necessary food requirements?[16] The only answer that seems to come forth is another question: What would they do if they were not farming? The spectre of unemployment seems

---

[15] So far in Viet-Nam's land reform over 100,000 farm families have been told what parcel of land they will receive. This program is actively supported by the official American groups. (Unpublished mimeographed letter of J. P. Gittinger, Agricultural Economist, USOM/Saigon.)

[16] Norman S. Buchanan and Howard S. Ellis, *Approaches to Economic Development* (New York: The Twentieth Century Fund, 1955), pp. 256-66.

to be at least as formidable a barrier as the introduction of the highly productive modern agricultural techniques.

A land use and land reform program for Viet-Nam that is development oriented must recognize the situation as it exists.

The farmer must be made sufficiently productive to permit his family to enjoy the comforts and advantages that modern technology can provide. This expansion of productivity of the farmer is also necessary to meet the food needs of a rapidly expanding population, particularly in the cities. As long as the farmer is a third-class citizen, he will remain an unproductive and generally uninterested citizen dreaming about some miracle which will open to him the wonders of the Western world.

The land-use programs (including land ownership programs and land taxation programs) must provide incentives, including a general atmosphere of moving on to the new rather than an effort to capture a dream of the past.[17] The picture of the new is land, machines, and men combined efficiently and productively to carry out farming operations. This will call for a rather rapid reduction of the number of persons earning a living directly from the land as the productivity of each person on the land increases. This situation would permit the country to feed increasing numbers of persons engaged in professions, service industries, manufacturing, transportation, and government.

This obviously is not the future which should be expected to develop out of appeals to owning your own little plot of ground and cultivating it as in the past with some minor improvements in seed and maybe some provision for the distribution of fertilizers. This type of program is not development oriented because it does not a) seem to be a reasonable approach to the new aspirations of the peasant now that he knows of the opportunities that can be his, and b) because it does not provide the income and production base that modern agriculture is capable of developing. To go through the stage of somewhat more efficient family plot farming before entering into the stage of commercial farming is similar to insisting that gas lights be introduced in the village before electricity is used or that 19th century factories be reproduced rather than modern factories.[18] The intermediate steps are not needed and in many ways are false steps. By taking them, you are to an extent discouraging the people involved, for they fully realize what they are doing does not require the best of them since other men in other places are doing the same job in a much more efficient fashion.

---

[17] Charles P. Kindleberger, *Economic Development* (New York: McGraw-Hill, 1958), pp. 29-34, 63-65.

[18] In *The Strategy of Economic Development* (New Haven: Yale University Press, 1958), Albert O. Hirschman refers to the desirability of forces that press for development. These forces arise when agriculture is developed on a 20th century basis rather than a Western 19th century basis.

The more exacting the process of production is, the more the activity forces the personal discipline which is such a necessary requirement for economic advance.

It was mentioned before that fear of the great expansion of the unemployed, which would result from efficient agriculture in the modern sense, has been a strong deterrent to a land use and general agricultural program which would be development oriented. There is no doubt that the agricultural program (and the land reform program in particular) in progress in Viet-Nam was strongly influenced by the desire to absorb the idle and the unemployed into subsistence agriculture. The adoption of this particular approach to solve the problem of unemployment has political and cultural roots.[19] It is obvious that dissatisfied people and unemployed persons cause less trouble when away from the capital and scattered over the countryside. The weight given to this relationship in setting agricultural policy should not be neglected during these days of political turmoil. But who would say that it provides a sound basis for future development? Certainly the procedures used 500 years ago or a device to make governing less troublesome is not a particularly suitable basis for the development of a program sufficiently dynamic to provide the framework for catching up with the rest of the world.

In practice this has worked out in Viet-Nam to a program that can be summarized as follows:

1. A land reform aimed at establishing small farmer-owned acreages.

2. Expansion into new territories, making use of the village organization of ancient Viet-Nam.

3. Limited development of resources to help the independent farmer; e.g., cooperatives, seed and stock distribution, agricultural education, and extension.[20]

4. Practically exempting land from taxation.

In most aspects this is not an unusual program. It is, in fact, the one which has been most frequently recommended by American and other free world agricultural advisors. It has also been rather widely accepted as the free world's answer to the Communist agricultural program. Because a program along these lines has been propagandized by many and because it has gained rather wide acceptance, it is difficult for one

---

[19] "Even before Champa was defeated (1471), mandarins and nobles had long sent 'vagabonds' and landless peasants into the fabulous south." Bittinger, *op. cit.*, p. 160.

[20] USOM/Saigon, *Activity Report for June 30, 1954 through June 30, 1956*, pp. 18-31.

such as myself, who is not an agriculturalist, to conclude that it is a bad program. Nevertheless, this is the direction which my analysis takes.

III.

The outlines of a land-use and agricultural program which I would recommend as an alternative for the awakening countries is as follows:

1. Initiation of a crash program aimed at educating those who wish to learn modern agricultural methods and how to operate and repair agricultural machinery. While this program would be open to everyone, participants would be required to maintain high performance standards in order to continue. These persons would also be paid a substantial salary while participating in the program.

2. The state would start a program of buying up land areas and forming farms of sufficient size for sound commercial agriculture. These farms would be sold under a program providing for annual payments. Those graduating from the agricultural program would be given first chance to purchase these farms. Also, provision would be made to assist in the financing of the machinery required.

3. In the industrial sector, priority would be given to the development of plants producing farm machinery. In the distribution and marketing sectors, priority would be given to those aspects most directly related to agriculture.

4. The taxes levied on land would be high. High taxes would take away a considerable portion of the additional product arising from the introduction of modern agricultural methods and at the same time force farmers using primitive methods to adopt modern techniques. Farmers not able to pay the land tax would have to sell their land to the government and go to work as outlined in point 5 below.

5. Persons relieved from performing agricultural activities would be placed on government payrolls to construct road, sewer, and other construction projects. In addition, they would benefit from evening training programs.[21] Most of the financing for this activity

---

[21] "So low is the productivity of Latin American farm workers . . . that it takes three and a half persons working on farms to produce what is contributed

would come from the increase of taxes assessed on agricultural land. Some of the financing could justifiably arise from deficits.

Agriculture must gradually change from a primitive and unproductive way of life for large masses of Viet-Nam's population and become an efficient member of the nation's industrial complex if those living on the farms are to enjoy the goods and services which are a part of modern life.[22] A program directly aimed at introducing modern agriculture and reducing the number of people working on farms must be the cornerstone of the land-use program. No other plan can be accepted for it is not possible to escape from the realities of the current scene. To those who see it objectively, that scene is one of recognizing the superiority of Western production methods and a desire of all peoples to participate in the modern life which provides the Western way of living with its opportunities and enjoyments.

All land reform programs in countries similar to Viet-Nam must have as a primary aim a reduction in the number of people on the farms. The farming activity of the nation must go step by step straight toward commercial agriculture. If this is done, agriculture becomes a dynamic element in preserving social stability during change and furthering industrialization.

As agriculture becomes commercialized, the market for manufactured goods expands in the countryside from higher farm incomes and in the city because lower food prices will leave the city family with more money to spend on goods and services. These expanded markets would provide another help to the nation's development program. Also, a reduction in farm population would permit the collection of increased property taxes.[23]

The great error that has been committed by persons fostering a land program like the one being implemented in Viet-Nam is that they have acted as though the land-labor ratio in agriculture is identical to some sort of a job-labor ratio. This, indeed, is not the situation because the number of jobs that need doing is very great. The labor needed to do them is presently absorbed in carrying on primitive agriculture.

to the national wealth by one person engaged in other activities." United Nations Economic Commission for Latin America, *New York Times,* 19 May 1959. Observers have often estimated that the marginal productivity of agricultural workers of Asia is frequently near zero.

[22] Economic development may be not so much "one of economic growth within an existing framework but the replacement of one civilization by another." A. K. Cairncross, "Economic Development and the West," *Three Banks Review,* December 1957, p. 31, quoted by Edward S. Mason in *Economic Planning in Underdeveloped Areas* (New York: Fordham University Press, 1958).

[23] Aaron M. Sakolski, *Land Tenure and Land Taxation in America* (New York: Robert Schalkenbach Foundation, 1957), pp. 259-61.

COMMENT

Nguyen Phu Duc

For an examination of the land-use program in Viet-Nam, we should take into consideration the economic background of the country, the repercussions of the war which lasted from 1946 to 1954, and the partition of the country along the 17th parallel.

Dean Lindholm interpreted the land reform program in Viet-Nam as an effort aimed mainly at establishing small farmer-owned acreages.

In Southern Viet-Nam* before the war, 1 per cent of the owners, holding more than 100 hectares, claimed title to some 49 per cent of the total rice land. After the Armistice, South Viet-Nam received an influx of nearly 900,000 refugees from Communist North Viet-Nam, most of whom were farmers. In addition, the National Army has been reduced from the war level of 320,000 men to 150,000. Many of the soldiers thus released had been landless tenants and were to be provided productive activities when they returned to civilian life.

The land distribution program, therefore, helped to absorb into the economic life of the nation this mass of more than one million people, representing approximately 10 per cent of the total population of South Viet-Nam. At the same time it prevented a further increase in the urban population, which rose enormously during the war years.

Dean Lindholm interpreted the rural exodus in Viet-Nam as based fundamentally on a "deep feeling that life on the land is no longer meaningful and that the city somehow symbolizes the new possibilities open to all people now that the secrets of the West are known." In reality, the rural exodus in Viet-Nam was due to the destruction and insecurity in the countryside during the war, and the booming trade and business in the cities created by the presence of the French Expeditionary Corps of 300,000 men.

As is well known, the war in Viet-Nam was characterized by large-scale guerrilla warfare conducted mainly in the countryside, coupled with the "scorched earth" strategy of the Viet-Minh. The principal theater of active warfare was in North Viet-Nam. Therefore, the large cities in general, and those in Southern Viet-Nam in particular, became the security zone in the country. As a result, the urban population of Southern Viet-Nam swelled from 7 per cent of the total Southern population in 1939 to 35 per cent by the end of the war. The population of Saigon-Cholon, which was 498,000 in 1943, representing 9 per cent of the Southern population, rose in 1953 to 1,614,000 or 27 per cent of the Southern population. In the beginning of 1955 the

---

* In these remarks, "Southern Viet-Nam" designates the part of Viet-Nam formerly called "Cochinchina" by the French; "South Viet-Nam" is the territory of the Republic of Viet-Nam, south of the 17th parallel.

population of Saigon-Cholon increased to 1,900,800 with the arrival of the refugees from North Viet-Nam.

Consequently, during the war at least 20 per cent of the population shifted from the agricultural segment to the business and utilities segment favored by the French war expenditures. Before the war, agriculture accounted for 62 per cent of the national income. It fell to less than 30 per cent at the end of the war, in a country which remains agricultural.

The decline in production was accompanied by a rocketing rise in prices and salaries. In 1957 the index of wholesale prices rose to about 30 times that of 1939. The retail price index, on the other hand, reached about 70 times that of 1939, tax rates having tended to drop.

When Viet-Nam returned to a peacetime economy, it became necessary to reverse the trend by returning more people to the agricultural segment. The land distribution, which is a part of the land reform program, should be viewed against this background.

By limiting land holding to 100 hectares, more land was made available for distribution, thus providing job opportunities for landless tenants, or smaller landholders.

From the political standpoint, the formula is: "The land must belong to him who cultivates it."

The objectives of sound commercial agriculture advocated by Dean Lindholm, when he suggested larger farmer-owned acreage, have in fact been pursued in Viet-Nam through the organization of agricultural cooperatives.

Since 1954, 142 agricultural cooperatives have been formed, 40 of which are for rice growers. Each cooperative has many hundreds of members. The cooperative of Go-Cong, for instance, covers no less than 40 villages. These cooperatives have modern equipment, warehouses, and husking mills available to their members. They are also in a better position than individual farmers to obtain loans from the National Agricultural Credit Organization created in 1957.

Besides land distribution, the land reform program in Viet-Nam aims at the reclamation of lands abandoned during the war and the opening up of new lands for cultivation. Under the direction of the Land Development Board, 15,356 hectares have been reclaimed at Cai-San, An-Xuyen, Ba-Xuyen, and the Plaine des Jones. From 1957 to 1959, 48,000 hectares were cleared. Of the 30,805 hectares put into cultivation, 22,542 were devoted to rice growing and the balance to industrial crops and vegetables.

Whenever possible, land cultivation is done in large farming units. Since April 1957, 44 land development centers have been established, covering 23,086 hectares of land. The centers occupy areas ranging from 100 to 500 hectares, with some large projects covering between 3,000 and 4,000 hectares.

The usefulness of a mechanized agriculture has not been overlooked. By December 1958, more than 300 tractors and bulldozers were available to farmers through the Agricultural Mechanical Directorate. This same agency was responsible in 1958 for the clearing, plowing, and disking of 28,723 hectares, resulting in substantial savings. It is hoped that further mechanization will be financially feasible.

Dean Lindholm suggested giving priority in the industrial sector to the development of factories producing farm machinery. Under present circumstances a more practical approach would be to import farm machinery and to direct effort, as the government of Viet-Nam is doing, toward the industrial production of items for local consumption (i.e., textiles, glassware, sugar, paper, etc.) whose imports are responsible for the deficit of our balance of trade.

The substantial rise of land taxes suggested by Dean Lindholm "to prod farmers using primitive methods into adopting modern techniques," could be adopted only with great difficulties unless increased production had already been achieved. This recommendation supposes also that a drop in the price of rice, as predicted by Lindholm, would not seriously affect the income of farmers. Actually, the most welcome consequence of an increased agricultural production will be a more favorable balance of trade. Toward this end and aside from undertakings to increase production in rice and rubber, Viet-Nam's two main exports, efforts are being made along two major fronts. First, there has been an attempt to diversify agricultural production to include jute, ramie, coffee, tea, etc.; secondly, efforts have been made to increase exports as well as to reduce imports on some agricultural items. Indeed, the possibilities of a shrinking foreign market, for rice in particular, are kept in mind. This consciousness stems from the knowledge that Mainland China, a rice importer in the past, may export a considerable tonnage of rice within the near future.

Dean Lindholm also raised the very pertinent problem of unemployment which would result from the modernization of agriculture, or rather, which will succeed the chronic underemployment in the countryside. The problem arises also from an expanding population. However, the population is not expanding quite as fast as indicated by Dean Lindholm. The rate of growth is 1.8 per cent per year, according to recent figures. For the solution of the problem, Dean Lindholm advocated only public works projects financed by higher land taxes and possibly by budgetary deficits. Public works projects and deficit financing, in my view, can be only a temporary solution. Although he pictured the current scene as one which should improve agriculture by Western production methods, Dean Lindholm did not mention as an answer that a certain measure of industrialization is apparently needed.

In South Viet-Nam, for example, industrialization is not the catch-word for economic development; on the contrary, the five-year plan gives priority to agriculture. However, a gradual setting up of light conversion industries is being undertaken in an attempt to reduce the imports of items for mass consumption, and to absorb the portion of population which can be released from the overcrowded agricultural segment. This may insure a balanced growth for an underdeveloped economy, even for a country considered to have an "agricultural vocation."

Part IV

FINANCE
IN VIET-NAM

American Aid
and Its Financial Impact

This article is one of several reprinted with permission from the book "Viet-Nam—The First Five Years," published by the Michigan State University Press in 1960.

Here Professor Lindholm summarizes the American aid program from its inception up to the renewal of serious internal difficulties in Viet-Nam. It is a summary of the four years when Viet-Nam was almost a viable nation with substantial American economic and organizational assistance. We know today the effort failed. Some of the reasons for this failure become observable in this analysis.

Following the article are comments that point up the controversial nature of Professor Lindholm's discussion. The first commentator, David Hotham, is a correspondent for the London Times and Economist in the Far East. Tran Van Kien, the next commentator, is an assistant professor of economics at the National Institute of Administration in Saigon. The last commentator, John M. Hunter, is an international economist currently with the Ford Foundation in the Argentine and professor of economics at Michigan State University.

American aid to Viet-Nam has been aimed at developing a politically and economically viable nation that would be able to meet the needs and aspirations of both the illiterate farmer and the graduate of a great French university. To accomplish these aims, law and order had to be established and the possibility of a Communist invasion had to be reduced.

In its allocations the United States Congress has recognized, if not over-recognized, the military support phase of the aid program. This is apparent in Table 1, which shows total aid granted for three major categories—military support, refugee aid, and economic and technical assistance—during the three fiscal years 1954-55, 1955-56, and 1956-57, together with estimates for 1957-58.

TABLE 1

AMERICAN AID, 1954-58*

(in thousands of dollars)

Fiscal Year	Military Support	Refugee Aid	Economic and Technical Assistance	Total
1957-58*	$155,000	....	$ 29,000	$184,000
1956-57	173,000	....	82,900	255,900
1955-56	109,000	$37,000	50,500	196,500
1954-55	234,800	55,785	29,715	320,300
Total	$671,800	$92,785	$192,115	$956,700
Per Cent of Total	69	9	22	100

* Totals for 1958 are tentative. A $25 million loan was also extended which would be added to the economic and technical assistance total of $50 million. In 1957-58 about 50 per cent of the economic and technical assistance total was allocated to the construction of a modern highway between Saigon and Bien Hoa.

SOURCE: Viet-Nam Desk, ICA, Washington.

As Table 1 indicates, two thirds of total American aid has been used to finance the redevelopment of the military forces. In addition, according to Table 2, which provides details of the 1956-57 American aid program, some 8 per cent of the total allocated for economic and technical assistance was used to develop the police forces ($5,786,640 plus $1,000,000 of the allocation for the National Institution of Administration). The amount has been large, but the task has also been formidable.

Refugee aid amounted to 10 per cent of the total, which was for the first two-year period under consideration. Of the total allocated for economic and technical assistance in 1956-57, $10 million (see Table 2) or about 12 per cent was used to support rural resettlement, which was largely a refugee-related program.

Economic and technical assistance received 22 per cent of total American aid during the period under consideration. The amount to be used for this purpose has steadily increased, while the allocations for refugees has dropped sharply. However, the amount spent for military assistance has shown little tendency to decrease.

The average annual total of American aid during this period has been $236.9 million. A large portion of this has been used to finance the purchase of consumer products from other countries. Viet-Nam's negative trade balance of about nine billion piasters is brought into

TABLE 2

ECONOMIC AND TECHNICAL ASSISTANCE
WITH ESTIMATED EXPENDITURE, FISCAL YEAR 1956-57
(in thousands of dollars)

AGRICULTURE AND NATURAL RESOURCES

Small water control systems	$ 1,374
Administration of agrarian reform	607
Land development (rural resettlement)	10,034
General livestock development	1,169
Development of marine fisheries	430
Agricultural extension and information	351
National Agricultural College and general training	687
Research in diversified crops	337
Agricultural credit and cooperatives	190
Agricultural economics and statistics	111
Total	$15,290

INDUSTRY AND MINING

Nong Son coal exploration survey	$ 56
Telecommunication development	719
Electric power development	843
Paper industry survey	25
Sugar industry survey	36
Industrial Development Center	10,000
General industrial survey	804
Rural water supply development	417
Saigon-Cholon water system survey	122
Handicraft development	99
Total	$13,121

TRANSPORTATION

Highways and bridges	$20,694
Viet-Nam railway system	4,413
Saigon port loan	229
Waterways of Viet-Nam	298
Improvement and expansion of aeronautical ground facilities	3,006
Total	$28,640

LABOR

Labor school	$ 200
Labor ministry organization	40
Total	$ 240

HEALTH AND SANITATION

Malaria eradication program	$ 1,231
Medical and allied education	3,554
Health services development	1,410
Total	$ 6,195

EDUCATION

Technical vocational education	$ 883
Elementary education	1,002

Secondary education	480
Teacher training and higher education	1,450
Adult literacy training	350
Textbook development and special services	204
Total	$ 4,369

PUBLIC ADMINISTRATION

Civil police administration	$ 5,787
Training civil tax expert	8
Fellowship on taxation and public finance	150
National Institute of Statistics	214
National Institute of Administration and MSU administrative support	2,037
Travel costs for Vietnamese scholarship students to and from Viet-Nam	100
Total	$ 8,296

GENERAL AND MISCELLANEOUS

Development of government information facilities	$ 779
National radio network	889
General program administration	5,072
Total	$ 6,740
GRAND TOTAL FOR 1956-57 PROGRAM	$82,891

approximate balance by dollars made available by the American aid program.

Viet-Nam's imports for 1956 were concentrated in the consumer area, with about 40 per cent consisting of textiles, food, drink, and tobacco. The Bureau of Customs shows that about 17 per cent of the 1956 imports were classified as investment goods. If this classification presents an accurate picture, then 83 per cent of the imports are consumer-type imports or are used up in the productive process—for example, imports such as coal and oil.

These quantities of imports and approximately these types of imports are necessary to permit the Vietnamese government to spend considerably more than it collects in taxes, while avoiding conditions very likely to cause disruptive inflation. The procedure used in extending aid was developed in Western Europe during the days of the Marshall Plan and was transferred to Asia as an appropriate administrative device. The device has not worked particularly well, primarily because the governments that have received aid have not been able to balance their normal operating budgets; and, therefore, the aid is operating budget support rather than investment support, as was the situation in Western Europe.

One important reason why Viet-Nam in its operating budget relies on American aid counterpart funds (piasters arising from the sale of imports financed with American aid dollars) to directly supply 50 per cent of its revenues, and indirectly another 25 to 30 per cent, is that the Vietnamese government is carrying on activities that are far above its fiscal capability.[1] The largest of these expenditures is the budgeted amounts for the armed forces. In addition to this expenditure, which is equal to about 50 per cent of the total national budgeted expenditures, there are those expenditures related to administration and operation of all the various projects listed in Table 2. Each of these, with the exception of $150,000 listed under public administration, is at least indirectly a government revenue spending program. The increase of the money value of the productivity likely to arise from these projects is uncertain, and the ability of the government to tap this increased productivity, if and when it does arise, is even less certain. The end result of an American aid program of this type is quite different from that undertaken in Western Europe.

In Viet-Nam the abandonment or reduction of American aid would leave behind an inflated government budget, with some expansion of productivity and skills instead of largely modern production facilities, as was the case in Western Europe. Vietnamese leaders often speak of the desirability of the type of impact which American aid had in France, or perhaps of the end result of Russian and Chinese aid in Red Viet-Nam, and contrast this with the impact of American aid in Free Viet-Nam. An impact similar to that realized by American aid to Europe could be enjoyed under present conditions *if* the economic and technical aid were concentrated in only a few areas, such as land and power development, *if* the military personnel were to consist largely of part-time soldiers, *if* these military savings were funneled into economic and technical assistance, *if* the government of Viet-Nam developed an effective individual savings program, and *if* a tax program were developed which brought in 11 to 15 per cent of Viet-Nam's gross national product, instead of 6 to 8 per cent as is presently the situation.[2] This sort of program makes a lot of sense, and many persons of good will in Viet-Nam and the United States favor a development of the American aid program along these lines.

As to the financial impact of American aid, it is the large portion of funds used to pay the Vietnamese army and other military costs that has been frequently misunderstood by correspondents in Viet-Nam. This misunderstanding has led to statements such as: American aid should be used to finance industrial machinery, not so many new cars; it should be used to produce producer goods, not consumer goods.

To understand why things have worked out as they have, one can consider, as an example, what happens when the Vietnamese army

---

[1] Somewhat more than 50 per cent of the tax revenues of the national government arise from custom duties applied to imports financed with American aid dollars.

[2] Taken from tax studies of the State Secretary of Finance of Viet-Nam.

needs 35 million piasters to pay its troops. To provide budgetary support for this expenditure, the American government has made a credit of one million dollars available to the National Bank of Viet-Nam in the form of a deposit in a commercial bank in the United States. (One dollar at the official rate of exchange equals 35 piasters.)

In exchange for this increase of its dollar holdings, the National Bank credits the account of American aid (ICA in Saigon) for 35 million piasters. A check for this amount is then presented to the Secretary of State for Finance by American aid officials in Saigon, and he deposits it in the Vietnamese Treasury, thereby increasing the balance of the national government by 35 million piasters.

Because soldiers are paid with currency, and not by check, the Treasury generally demands currency in exchange for the check. The National Bank provides this currency either from currency it has received from commercial banks in exchange for deposit credits, from currency it has received from the sale of foreign exchange, or with new currency (coins and paper money) which it issues. After the Treasury receives this currency, it makes it available to army paymasters as needed; and, as it is paid out, the National government's balance at the Treasury decreases accordingly. The currency in the hands of the army paymasters, and later of the soldiers, increases by a like amount.

The soldiers and the suppliers for the army spend a considerable portion for food, drink, and clothing, and, in addition, purchase trinkets, cigarettes, and transportation. The providers of these goods and services replenish their stocks by purchasing new supplies from domestic and foreign sources; for example, they purchase tea from wholesalers who buy from domestic producers and canned milk from wholesalers who buy from foreign producers.

The wholesaler can use piasters to make his tea purchases, but to buy his canned milk supply he must first exchange his piasters for dollars, francs, or some other foreign exchange. If he wishes to purchase a supply of canned milk costing $1,000, he must pay 35,000 piasters to his commercial bank. Eventually, the commercial bank must transfer 35,000 piasters to the National Bank for the $1,000 needed by its wholesaler customer.

When the wholesaler begins to make arrangements to import more canned milk, he prevents a decrease in the quantity of goods that will be available for sale in Viet-Nam: He is making certain that there will be canned milk to meet the demands and, in doing this, he performs the first step in seeing that there will be goods on the market to meet the piasters offered in the market in exchange for goods.

When the wholesaler makes his piaster payment for the dollar exchange, he gives up a considerable portion of the piasters he has received from various customers for canned milk. The economic want for canned milk has been satisfied, and the piasters searching for goods have been reduced by this amount. When the commercial bank makes the payment to the National Bank, the cycle of this flow of piasters is complete. The piasters were put into and taken out of circulation by the National Bank.

The types of goods which the wholesalers and manufacturers import are restricted somewhat by the regulations set by the Vietnamese government, but basically the types of goods which they import are items that can be sold.

Therefore, the use of American aid is determined by how the Vietnamese use their incomes and their savings. The fact that a large portion of the Vietnamese imports financed with American aid are either consumer goods or raw materials used rather directly to meet consumer demands is an indication that the Vietnamese people desire these goods, for they have shown their desire by their willingness to use their piasters to purchase them.

Should the situation change in Viet-Nam so that wholesalers find it difficult to sell radios or gasoline but easy to sell sugar-refining equipment or road-building machinery, they would, of course, request permits to import these products. Should this new situation arise, the piaster supply, which was increased when the Treasury presented the ICA check to the National Bank, would be decreased to its former level when the National Bank received piasters spent by the Vietnamese to increase the productive capacity of their country rather than to meet their demands for consumer goods.

If the people of Viet-Nam do not voluntarily refrain from spending their current income or former accumulations on consumer goods which must be imported, or if the government does not reduce its ability to do this through tax collections and a restrictive monetary policy, American aid is not available to acquire producer goods. That is, American aid is not available to acquire producer goods unless the government of Viet-Nam wishes to increase drastically all the problems associated with economic controls and a deterioration of its currency. As a matter of fact, the latter alternative is really not available, for American taxpayers are providing the dollars which ICA/Washington deposits in a U.S. commercial bank in order to prevent inflation in Viet-Nam during this critical period of reconstruction.

COMMENTARY:
David Hotham on Lindholm

No degree of industry can ever be introduced into Viet-Nam as long as the only goods that are imported are ones that can be resold. What importer, as Lindholm implies, is going to order equipment for a textile factory or a steel plant, and who, in a nation whose population is 80 per cent peasants, is going to buy such equipment?

If one depends simply on the normal working of supply and demand, industry in Viet-Nam, virtually nonexistent at present, can never be developed. Even in the United States, where this method did work and where there was an almost unlimited supply of private capital, it took fifty or more years for industry to develop. Rapid industrialization, however, is urgently needed in Free Viet-Nam because of the Communist menace to the north. How, then, can this new nation, lacking private capital, develop an industrial sector, and do so rapidly?

By far the best and quickest way to introduce some industry is to create state-owned industries. There are many difficulties in doing this, such as the fact that most of the existing industry in the south is owned by the French or Chinese; however, this amounts to nothing more than a few cigarette factories, breweries, and rice mills.

If there could be a large influx of private capital invested in Viet-Nam, it might be possible to create industry without infringing on the principle of private enterprise. But there are two factors which render this extremely difficult. First, foreign investors, despite the law encouraging investment, have not hastened to put their money into a country whose political future is so uncertain. (It is significant that there has been almost no private American investment in Free Viet-Nam.) Secondly, the Vietnamese are not in any hurry to repeat a pattern whereby their industries are foreign-owned in the future.

American aid has financed many excellent and well-conceived programs in Viet-Nam: the resettlement of refugees, the anti-malaria and anti-trachoma work, the agricultural improvements, the supplying of thousands of buffaloes, the restocking of fishponds, the reclaiming of waste land, the research on the high plateau of the interior, the invaluable long-term work on statistics, taxation, and other fields, and the training in administration and the introduction of American methods and ideas carried out by Michigan State University. Also, it cannot be denied that the counterpart fund system of aid has helped to avert inflation, which was so fatal in Kuomintang China.

It is not the details, but the main lines, of the aid program which are wrong, because they negate the effect of the excellent activities enumerated. If Viet-Nam were a country such as Iceland, isolated and with no serious Communist danger, all would be well. However, Viet-

Nam is in intimate competition with Communists next door—co-existence at the very closest quarters. Unless the main lines of the American aid program are right, democracy shall not win the Vietnamese. The exaggerated overemphasis on the army, the lack of housing in a country where there is terrible poverty and misery (particularly in Saigon, where one fourth of the population lives), the quasi-paralysis which afflicts the land reform program, the failure to do anything effective about chronic unemployment and underemployment, and the failure to introduce industry—these are the big things which count in the small cold war north and south of the 17th parallel, in which propaganda counts as much as anything. The best propaganda will be facts which the Vietnamese can see. The vast majority of the population of Free Viet-Nam, seeing $250 million or so pouring into their little country every year, naturally asks where all this money is spent. And the Communists help them to speculate.

Why are Americans so reluctant to help underdeveloped countries to industrialize? Is there some fear that the creation of an industrial proletariat will encourage communism? Or is it that Americans do not want the countries in question to become economically independent too quickly? Granted that hasty and ill-considered industralization in any country is a serious mistake, one might still ask: Has the extraordinarily rapid industrialization of Puerto Rico, for example, been wrong?

In the case of Free Viet-Nam, many eminent and hard-headed American businessmen have reported on the good prospects for a varied selection of light industries. The aid program should be adapted to financing such industries and the other things which need doing. Why should economic aid not be given in the form of factories, with American technicians to set them up? If there is some good economic or political reason for not doing so, Americans should know what it is.

COMMENTARY:
Tran Van Kien on Lindholm

Of all the aid programs given to Viet-Nam by the Free World (UN assistance, Colombo Plan, etc.), the American program is by far the most important. It would not be difficult, therefore, to draw a balance sheet of results achieved by the latter.

The procedure followed in Viet-Nam was the same as that of the Marshall Plan in Europe; that is why a comparison of the two programs is invariably made whenever an evaluation of results in Viet-Nam is attempted. The outcome of such a comparison is necessarily unfavorable.

Although the Marshall Plan brought about Europe's economic recovery, the Vietnamese economy remains, after eight years of assistance, entirely dependent upon American aid. This difference in results is not caused so much, as has been contended, by the fact that the Vietnamese government used the aid as "budget support" instead of "investment support" but rather by differences in the structures of the two economies and also by the political situation in Viet-Nam.

In Europe it was the commercialized-aid formula that successfully cured the dollar shortage caused by Europe's efforts to rebuild its productive facilities which had been ravaged by the war. Thus, European producers were able to use national currencies to pay for equipment needed to put existing plants and factories back into operation; the proceeds in local currencies were then turned over to European governments, which used them to finance their investment programs. This combined effort by private business and governments enabled Europe to become economically independent within a short time. American aid provided exactly what European producers needed.

The case of Viet-Nam is different. It is true that few investment efforts were made because of budget deficits, as has been demonstrated; but nothing has been done by businessmen either. The Vietnamese economy is not at all comparable to that of Europe, which already had a productive apparatus tested and proven by several decades of industrialization, and which also had businessmen and industrialists who knew what their needs were. Furthermore, the political and military situation which prevailed at the time in Viet-Nam was not favorable to any reconstruction efforts. The Vietnamese government was too busily engaged in fighting a war to think of encouraging businessmen in productive investments that would be useful to the country's economy. In addition, the necessity of maintaining a certain standard of living among the population, in order "to defeat communism with prosperity," demanded immediate results, which long-term investment programs could not provide.

For these reasons, American aid dollars were not used for investment purposes but to finance imports of consumer goods. In this respect, American aid achieved notable results, enabling the Vietnamese government to deal successfully with problems of the hour. The aid contributed greatly to the preservation of a suitable standard of living for the population and, thus, it is well to stress, to the care and improvement of that form of capital of vital importance for economic development: human capital.

But once the military and political phase has been left behind, the time has come to place the nation's economy on a healthier and more stable basis. The problem is the efficient use of American funds within the framework of present procedures, which would be difficult to change, so that the economy would remain viable when that aid is discontinued.

Toward this end, Viet-Nam should have a productive apparatus suitable to its needs and capabilities. Concentrated efforts in a few limited fields—agriculture and power—should be only a first phase soon to be succeeded by the gradual establishment of a few industries. It is true the country's partition, which meant the loss of the greater part of its natural resources, has greatly diminished its industrial potential; but a purely agricultural economy would be subjected to too much instability and would not have the means for absorbing surplus manpower resulting from the mechanization of agriculture and population growth. Priority should be given to those industrial sectors producing for the domestic market and using local resources instead of imported raw materials.

To do this, considerable investment efforts would have to be made by the government as well as private persons. It would, however, be useless—even dangerous—to reduce military expenditures too far as long as the Communist threat persists. The main effort must then come from individuals. The government, on the other hand, would have to develop, as has been suggested, a private savings program and at the same time take suitable measures to encourage and induce the productive effort, particularly imports of capital goods using aid funds. These measures would be all the more necessary because businessmen are inclined to import consumer goods which will bring them profits rather than capital goods. There is the added reason that a fall in imports would mean a decrease in counterpart funds used to finance government operations, as these funds come from payments made by importers. Of all these measures, only one might be mentioned—that toward private foreign investments, which has already been considered by the government and deserves to be carried out more thoroughly. Foreign capital flowing into certain well-defined sectors would be a useful addition to the available pool of domestic savings, which is small, as is always the case with a low-per-capita-income economy. Foreign capital would serve as the needed initial impulse to raise national income, and therefore savings. Foreign capital would also free a portion of national income, which is then available for consumer goods imports; and thus the necessity of subjecting the people to as severe an austerity program as the one prevailing in the Communist zone would be circumvented. Finally, in the form of long-term investments, foreign capital would provide substitutes for American aid when the latter stops.

Thus, to the extent that it can give Viet-Nam economic independence within the interdependence of the Free World, American aid will have achieved its goal.

COMMENTARY:

John M. Hunter on Lindholm

Foreign aid should be viewed by its top administrators and the United States Congress much as a corporation views its research expenditures: These expenditures are a necessary, integral part of development. Boards of corporations appropriate sums for such activity, knowing full well that the returns may be nebulous. Researchers, especially in any given period of time, may produce nothing of direct value. They may produce harmful results (e.g., patents that must be "buried"), or they may produce small or great immediate or future benefits whose values are not immediately estimable. They may produce nothing but negative results, but these, too, can be extremely valuable.

In many ways, aid programs are analogous; the same philosophy is applicable, if not necessary. The objectives of foreign aid are more or less clearly defined in the broad objectives of United States foreign policy, but aid on as broad a scale as Americans know it (and as it is apt to develop in the present political and economic world) is something shockingly new to them. Americans have not even a long history of colonial administration (not the same problem, but experience here would be helpful) to assist them. Under these programs, they literally project thousands of United States citizens into parts of the world about whose geography they knew little ten to twenty years ago. Foreign cultures, social structures, economic organization, and values were, and are, an even greater enigma to them. Individually and collectively, the people are improperly prepared to carry out the tasks the world situation assigns to them. "Learning by doing" is the essence of the physical scientist's laboratory; much of the American operation in the field of technical assistance is essentially the same.

Not only are they relative newcomers to the foreign scene, but they have no great body of knowledge to which they can turn for guidance even in their own culture. Basically, aid programs and technical assistance are designed to manipulate governments and something glibly called "public opinion" in nation after nation, as if Americans really understood these things.[3]

Like it or not, much of foreign aid will be of an experimental nature. Recognizing this explicitly would be wise administration. Making this a part of the aid philosophy, and effectively incorporating it into operating administration, would contribute substantially to the

---

[3] Perhaps this could be put more palatably, but aid programs *are* a part of U. S. foreign policy which *must* have geopolitical objectives. Even the more physically oriented projects (e.g., improving egg production of chickens) are a part of the "battle for the minds of men."

aid program. First of all, failures of particular projects would not be regarded necessarily as personal failures of their advocates or administrators, but rather as one of the expected costs of experimentation. Honest reporting of the failures, and the reasons therefore, could contribute much to the working paraphernalia of aid administrators who will be on the scene a long time. Failures in experimentation are frequently as valuable as successes and are sometimes necessary forerunners.

Further, more imaginative projects can and will be proposed. By removing some of the personal onus of failures, more imaginative projects can be undertaken—perhaps offering much greater returns but not now ventured because of risks of failure. Recognition of imaginative projects should do much to improve morale of personnel in the field and to attract more competent personnel.[4]

A genuine acceptance of this philosophy would free field personnel of many of the frustrations attendant upon the bureaucratic processes and would avoid the necessity for multiple clearances, multiple project justifications, multiple audits, etc., which so slow the processes that individuals who ultimately carry out projects are apt to lose enthusiasm or have their periods of assignment run out, or both. It is valuable training for the individual to discover that a technique will fail; it is also valuable to give responsibility and confidence to an individual (or a group) and let him work out his own salvation. Too much time is now spent in getting multiple approvals on everything in order to share responsibility in case of ultimate failure.

Accepting such a philosophy asks a great deal in a political democracy because it asks Congress to appropriate money with the confidence that wise people will spend wisely, and asks Congress to keep its "second guessing" to a minimum or to what is really more restrictive, an informed and responsible basis. Ultimately, then, the same is asked of the voters.

Presumably, this appeal could be made for nearly any governmental operation, but aid programs present a special case. Their unique elements are the immeasurability of results and the tremendous variations in economies, societies, and cultures in which they must operate—both of which make supervision from afar or on a part-time basis extraordinarily difficult, if not senseless.

---

[4] For example, a report and recommendations were censured by USOM in Saigon on the grounds that a proposal was "unorthodox." Whether the proposal was good or bad is not at issue; it was never considered because of the label affixed to it. Insistence on "orthodox" policy in "unorthodox" situations can be very expensive. An administrative philosophy effectively incorporating the idea of an experimental basis would permit field administrators room to operate outside the shackles of "orthodoxy."

Some increase in graft and diversion might occur and perhaps some foolish things would be undertaken, but the program as a whole would become more vibrant and dynamic and the gains would probably far outweigh the costs. The ship of state can run aground while all the crew is busy looking for minor leaks in the hold.

In evaluating foreign aid programs, the basic difficulty lies in the esoteric nature of the underlying objectives and the consequent difficulty of identifying results (output) for comparison with inputs. How do you measure successes and failures in the battles for men's minds?

Current evaluations lead to unfortunate biases in the selection of projects, and once projects are undertaken may give peculiar and undesirable slants to them. Favored projects are those with results that are concrete and can be pointed to, seen, and counted. The number of students in schools, the number of plows distributed, the number of people seeing United States-sponsored shows, etc., are measures of something and can be enumerated by an agency in reporting its activities. In so doing, the means and the ends may be confused. Also, these projects may not be the most productive in attaining the ultimate objectives. It may be much more important for an American technician to implant the seeds of "research-mindedness" in the mind of one Vietnamese than for the technician to produce five research jobs on his own. It is certainly of greater importance to convince one official of the necessity for widespread education than to seat one hundred youngsters in a new school. Yet, in the kinds of evaluations that now exist, the second project in each case above appears to be the better record.

One of the major contributors to this tendency is American unwillingness to seek long-run objectives on anything but short-run budgeting and planning. The kinds of things that foreign policy seeks to do through aid programs will not be done in a year; no appreciable progress may even be "visible" in that period of time.

If foreign aid programs are to be successful and efficient operations, Americans must stop trying to run them as if they were highway construction programs. They do not know as much about how to achieve desired results in the former as they do about laying concrete over various types of terrain. And they cannot conceivably lay "x" miles of foreign aid per year and expect to get sensible programs.

Financial Institutions
in Viet-Nam

*This lecture is taken from "Money, Banking, and Eco-
nomic Development," published in 1957 by the Cong-
Ban Press in Saigon. It explores the ways in which
financial institutions could best be organized to meet
the needs of an underdeveloped nation, particularly of
Viet-Nam. The problems considered go far beyond Viet-
Nam, though, because many developing nations—for
better or worse—find themselves with financial institutions that are copies of those in the United States or
Western Europe.*

The Treasury of Viet-Nam provides many services that are carried on by the Bureau of Internal Revenue or by the commercial banks
in countries not under the dominance of the financial institutional
arrangement prevalent in the Latin countries. To a considerable extent, the Treasury of Viet-Nam is a banking system that covers the
entire country. However, the services provided are aimed largely at
meeting the needs of the government. The facilities provided to meet
the needs of the private economy are limited to accepting deposits and
arranging for the transfer of these deposits.

In a country that is in the process of expanding its per capita income and the monetary portion of its economic activity as is Viet-Nam,
it is desirable that the financial institutions carry on the necessary
financial functions with the minimum amount of waste of the scarcest
of all resources—trained and honest personnel.

The system of Treasury such as exists in Viet-Nam is a very
old procedure that has been largely eliminated by forward-looking
countries. The reasons for the tendency to abandon the Treasury
system are many; but more than likely, the development of communi-
cation procedures—the telephone and the telegraph—and the development of bookkeeping machines were very important. The basic
weakness of the Treasury system is that it requires the establishment
of an institution to carry on only the business of the government. But

the Treasury is not even suited to perform all government business, for the Treasury is not equipped to handle the government central banking functions or, for that matter, a government program aimed at providing aid to agriculture. Also, the basic nature of the Treasury system is such that it discourages the use of checks in making payments, a development that for many reasons should be encouraged rather than discouraged.

If the Treasury system is in use, there must be established a sufficient number of sub-Treasuries to manage efficiently the finances of the government. In addition, individual institutions utilizing skilled personnel must be established to carry on specialized types of activity such as the lending of funds to farmers and others and the encouragement and development of consumer saving cooperatives. Finally, the Treasuries are not appropriate institutions to meet the commercial and industrial financial needs of the communities in which they are located. It is because the Treasury system encourages multiplicity and specialization of institutions that it is likely to lead to waste in the provision of necessary financial services.

In Saigon there is a tendency to operate banking institutions that specialize in foreign exchange banking. These institutions are again based upon a long tradition of specialization that is not easily violated. However, their specialized character is very likely to lead to waste in the provision of necessary financial services or, even worse, a failure to meet the minimum financial needs of the business community, the government, and the individuals.

By my mention of the foreign-exchange-specialized commercial banks of Saigon and the Treasury system, I do not intend to indicate that the personnel of these institutions are failing to perform very important functions. Rather, my purpose is to indicate some of the financial functions that must be carried on, and the adaptability of the present institutional arrangement to these functions.

The order in which I shall list the financial functions which should be performed may not correspond with the order of importance I would establish after a more complete consideration of the problem. However, at this time, they do represent the relative importance that I would assign. Also, I request that you keep in mind that each of the functions is related to the other functions, and therefore one function cannot be completely performed without the performance of the others.

The greatest need, as I see it, is to perform efficiently the many functions that must be combined to do a good job of gathering together the savings of small and large savers and making these savings available for investment in projects that will expand the productivity of Viet-Nam. This basic duty of the financial institutions of Viet-Nam can be performed properly only if the institutional arrangement effectively carries out the following functions:

1. Provides facilities convenient geographically and in organization of service to both the saver and the borrower.

2. Makes saving an attractive social goal in itself and particularly attractive when made in the form of accumulations in financial institutions; this function involves:

   a. Creating the general attitude that it is desirable to accumulate savings in a financial institution;

   b. Providing assurances plus proof of safety for the savings entrusted to the financial institution;

   c. Establishing procedures for setting a rate of return to the saver which corresponds with the realities of the money market—i.e., if 10 or 15 per cent per annum is the going rate, then savers must receive 8 or 13 per cent;

   d. Guaranteeing the easy withdrawal of savings and earnings on savings, and the removal of all possible doubt of the ability of the institution to pay the earnings assured or to cover withdrawal requests.

3. Provides that:

   a. Savings must be loaned only, or largely, to cover costs of productive investment;

   b. Loans must be made only on the basis of the expectation of repayment and must not be made on the basis of kinship unless that provides an additional guarantee of return;

   c. Loans once made must be closely supervised, and the borrower must be assisted by experts provided by the financial institution;

   d. Loan renewals and the period of the extension of the original loan must be related to the gestation period of the enterprise and must not be used to cover bad judgment.

   The types of institutions which have been developed in the countries of the world to carry out the basic function of gathering together and lending savings vary considerably, depending upon the historic background of the country and its current development. In Viet-Nam I would seriously suggest a financial institution that might be considered a department store of finance. The type of institution I visualize would have various departments to carry on ordinary domestic commercial banking, foreign exchange banking, agricultural lending, industrial lending, and consumer lending, and would accept business deposits, savings deposits, governmental deposits, etc. My reason for favoring this type of an institution is that it would make possible the very best use of the financial techniques available in Viet-Nam and would most successfully avoid the very undesirable possibility, because of the considerable pressures for additional financial services, of establishing institutions that cannot be properly staffed.

A second basic duty of the financial institutions of Viet-Nam is to provide the government with an efficient means of collecting and spending funds—to act as fiscal agent of the government. In Viet-Nam at the present time the National Bank performs some of these functions and the commercial banks a small additional portion, but basically they are performed by the Treasury.

I have already indicated that I believe this function of a fiscal agent should in time become one function of the department store type of credit institution. Performance of this fundamental function would have advantages, a few of which I shall outline briefly in just a moment. First permit me to point out some of the problems involved. If the government funds were handled by these financial department stores, the government would have to receive guarantees that its funds would not be falsely distributed or lost because of mismanagement. Also, the government would have to establish procedures for the most effective use of its funds. This would require that both the Secretary of State for Finance and the National Bank of Viet-Nam establish procedures for working with these department stores of finance to assure that their wishes are carried out. However, there is a silver lining to this dark cloud, for the suggested procedure would hasten effective government regulation.

Now the advantages of the procedure:

1. The funds accumulated by the government during the period of a year when receipts are greater than expenditures can earn an income for the government and can be used to finance private activities.

2. Offices to receive payments to the government and to cash government checks and warrants would become more numerous and therefore more convenient to the people and government administrative personnel while reducing government costs.

3. The government would develop the working opera-

tions with the financial community that are so important in carrying on cooperative relationships in all aspects of the government finance program.

4. The basic overall advantage of the procedure is that
   it eliminates the separation of government finance
   from that of nongovernment finance, which is a principal characteristic of the Treasury system now in use
   in Viet-Nam.

It will not be possible for me to spend more time on the functions
that should be performed by the financial institutions of Viet-Nam
or the type of organization best suited to the performance of these
functions in Viet-Nam. However, I believe we can all agree that to
have the two basic functions adequately performed, which I have briefly
described and considered, requires serious reconsideration of the type
of institutional organization that should be encouraged. In closing I
shall summarize the guidelines that seem to be useful in attacking this
very vital Vietnamese economic problem.

1. The personnel available that are trained in finance
   must be used in the most efficient manner. This more
   than likely requires the elimination of specialized
   financial institutions and the development of department store type institutions.

2. The major future work of financial institutions will be
   in the provision of domestic financial needs which have
   been badly neglected—both government and nongovernment. The efficiency with which this work is carried out will be very important in determining the
   productiveness of the Vietnamese economy.

3. Financial institutions must provide convenient and
   complete financial services to the people of all parts
   of the country. Again, the accomplishment of this necessary goal points to an institutional organization
   along the lines suggested above.

Powers of the National Bank of Viet-Nam

This lecture is also taken from "Money, Banking, and Economic Development in Free Viet-Nam," published in 1957 by the Cong-Ban Press in Saigon.

Professor Lindholm summarizes the development of the central bank with the advice of the Federal Reserve System of the United States.

I wish to discuss the heart of the powers given to the National Bank in Ordinance No. 48 of 31 December 1954. In any country the central bank's heart is its power to extend credit and to contract credit. This heart, in the case of the National Bank of Viet-Nam, is discussed in Chapter III of the Ordinance.

Central Bank Credit to Private Agencies
Chapter III, Section 2, Articles 50-55

The National Bank of Viet-Nam is not permitted to discount, rediscount, or buy and sell private credit instruments arising from medium- or long-term financing. The longest maturity that may be possessed by private notes against which the central bank may extend its credit— and then only as advances—is 365 days. This maximum length is available only if the notes arise from credit extended "by public or private credit establishments specialized in the granting of loans to crafts, industry, and agriculture and guaranteed by delivery to the National Bank." The credit extended by the National Bank on this basis may not exceed 50 per cent of the total of these evidences delivered to the National Bank. This type of National Bank credit availability can be very useful to new businesses not possessing the necessary liquidity to finance the purchase of the raw materials required in their operations and to credit institutions created to meet their needs. This power of the National Bank falls considerably short of what would be necessary if the National Bank were to make its credit available to specialized institutions to finance the purchase of equipment for the construction of production facilities.

The other type of regular private lending in which the National Bank may engage is described in Article 50, which provides for discount, rediscount, purchase and sale—and not just for advances—for 240 days and 120 days. The 240-day period is available if the note arose from "the production or the processing of agricultural products, or the products of mining, fishing or industry." The 120-day period is available if the note arose from financing related to "the export, import, purchase, sale or transport of immediately salable products or the storing in authorized places of non-perishable and properly insured products." The Board of Directors has complete power in establishing the terms under which these approved credits based on private security may be extended, including "the conditions of renewal of the loans, the margin of guarantees required."

I should mention here that this power to set the basis of renewal largely removes the restrictive feature of the relatively short maturity established in Article 50. However, the power to establish terms does not include the power to change the type of collateral which may be submitted to the National Bank for discounting, for purchase, or as the basis for an advance. Nevertheless, it must be remembered that if a businessman finds it easy to obtain credit to finance his inventories of raw materials and finished goods, he will acquire more funds to finance additional equipment and the like.

The central bank of a country is a lender of last resort, and provision for this is made in Paragraph 5 of Article 50 for the National Bank of Viet-Nam. It grants the Board of Directors power to extend advances to banks on any type of guarantee which the Board votes to be temporarily acceptable. If the bank receiving these advances is later unable to make repayment of the advance, it is not eligible for additional grants of central bank credit. The power granted here is very broad and certainly assures liquidity of banking enterprises—at least the first time they experience a crisis, and afterwards if they meet their obligations to the National Bank incurred during the first crisis.

It is in Article 52 that a very important principle related to the availability of central bank credit secured by private individuals or firms is established. The credit of the National Bank of Viet-Nam is available to the banks of Viet-Nam as a privilege and not as a right. Therefore, whenever the Board of Directors believes that the monetary or the economic stability of the country is threatened if additional central bank credit is extended, they may "refuse all requests for credits." And they may select particular banking institutions that have been functioning in a fashion which seems to be adding to the economic instability of the country and refuse them all credit.

It is of interest to us to note that Article 55 is a brief sermon exhorting the Board of Directors to act forthrightly in reducing the amount of central bank credit when Viet-Nam is suffering from severe inflationary pressures. However, we must realize that at present the National Bank is powerless to control the current inflationary pressures because neither does it possess securities which might be sold in the open market to reduce the money supply, nor are the commercial banks in debt to the National Bank or in need of the credit facilities. This situation exists because Viet-Nam has not as yet developed a money market through which the National Bank could carry on open market operations or securities to be used in this operation, and because of the excess liquidity of the banks of Viet-Nam. This excess is caused to a considerable extent by the inability of business firms to remit earnings and/or the failure of the government of Viet-Nam to collect adequate taxes and to control monopoly profits.

Central Bank Credit to Government
Chapter III, Section 3

It is in Section 3 of Chapter III that the conditions under which the National Bank of Viet-Nam may extend its credit to the government are set down. Each advance must be for a period of not over three months and must be represented by "negotiable Treasury bonds signed by the Secretary of State for Finance with a maximum term of three months." These securities are, however, renewable for periods of the same length. The government debt which may be purchased directly from the government by the National Bank of Viet-Nam is limited to these short-term government securities. The provisions of Ordinance No. 48 do not extend the right to make purchases of government securities from banks or other holders or to make loans or advances on the basis of collateral consisting of government securities. Thus the credit that the National Bank may extend directly to the government is limited to the direct purchase of short-term renewable securities. The amount of these securities which the government may sell the National Bank is limited to a cumulated total not greater than 25 per cent of the "State's own receipts recovered for the benefit of the State Budget in the course of the preceding year."

Although these provisions definitely place considerable restrictions on the financial assistance which the National Bank may extend the government, they do permit rather substantial grants of credit to the government at this time. If we assume that the revenues of the national government are 6.5 billion piasters (this total includes regional collections), the government could borrow 1.8 billion piasters. This is possible because, as of now, the government has borrowed only once from the National Bank, and this loan was repaid within a short period of time.

One other point related to government borrowing and the National Bank is of interest. Article 59 gives the National Bank the power to "endorse the Treasury bonds [and] place its unconditional guarantee thereon." If this is done and if when the bonds fall due the government is unable to repay the holders, the National Bank would be required to make the funds available. However, should this situation develop, if the government had not used up its loan limit, it would very likely borrow from the National Bank to meet these commitments. A question that is unanswered by Article 59 is whether a payment by the National Bank to cover the maturing debt would be considered a part of the 55 per cent borrowing limit. Logically this should be the case; but if it were, then the guarantee by the National Bank would be worthless if the borrowing of the government had reached the maximum established.

The National Bank is not directly given the power to purchase and sell government and other securities on the open market, although these powers are implied. For example, Chapter I, Section 2, Article 5, Paragraph 6 states in relation to the powers of the Director that "he initiates all acquisitions, sales, exchanges or transactions in transferable securities." And again Article 20, Paragraph 10 states in relation to the powers of the Board of Directors that "it fixes the conditions according to which the National Bank carries out credit operations." It decrees a list of securities admissible for these operations. These implied powers of the National Bank to purchase and sell securities on a very broad basis will, as the economy of Viet-Nam develops, become a very important portion of the heart of the National Bank. Here again, the 25 per cent limit is not mentioned, and it appears that the government could increase the credit extended to it by the National Bank by first offering its securities on the open market and having them purchased later by the National Bank.

Finally, I wish to mention that the National Bank, in Section 1 of Chapter III, is given rather complete authority over all transactions in foreign exchange and gold. The only article of this section is Article 49, which states that "the National Bank can acquire for a valuable consideration or free of charge, retain and sell gold and foreign exchange, and generally speaking utilize them." These powers are very broad, and when at some future date the foreign value of the piaster reaches a stable level, the National Bank will be able to use all the resources it possesses to maintain this level.

History of Money in Viet-Nam

The following lecture is also taken from "Money, Banking and Economic Development in Free Viet-Nam," a paperback book published in 1957 by the Cong-Ban Press in Saigon.

Here Professor Lindholm gives a history of Viet-Nam's money system up to the period of independence. The theme running through the lecture is that the money system of Viet-Nam was one of convenience to France but did not meet the needs of Viet-Nam.

I am very honored indeed to be selected by the Director of the National Institute of Administration to organize and to be the principal lecturer at this first course in money and banking to be offered at the NIA Evening School. I am also very glad that your government has decided to make available additional training for its experienced public servants who must now prepare themselves to assume positions of additional responsibility.

This course is appropriately titled "Money and Banking" both because money was utilized prior to the development of banking as we know it, and because banking today is so very closely associated with the character of the money in use.

The historical development of money is an interesting aspect of both the political and the economic history of the world, and also of individual nations. Although I do not pretend to be an expert on the historical development of the money of Viet-Nam, I still think it is more useful to discuss briefly the development of money in Viet-Nam than recount the French experience or the American experience from the *wampum* of the red Indians to the huge automatic machines that can sort and record to the proper account thousands of checks in a single day.

The money in use in Viet-Nam in the 1850's consisted of full-bodied metallic coins. The value of this money varied with the fluctuations in the value of the metal of which they were composed. The money included *nen vang* or gold bars, *nen bac* or silver bars, and *dong* or large copper coins. The ordinary transactions were largely completed with zinc *sapeks* or small bronze coins called *trinh*. To complete larger transactions, these *sapeks* circulated in strings of 60, which were known as *quan tien*.

The French army introduced the silver *piastre* which was known throughout the world as the Mexican dollar. This coin was also full-bodied, which meant that its value was determined by the value of the metal out of which it was made. After the introduction of the *piastre* (piaster), there were two types of money that were in common use in making exchanges of the more important type—the strings of sapeks and the piaster. These two types of money had a fluctuating exchange rate which moved, of course, with changes in the value of the metal of which they were composed.

I noticed the other day that 8 strings equaled one piaster back in 1886, while in 1898 one piaster was worth but 6 strings. It is of interest to note that, at this time, prices rose in Viet-Nam because the price of rice was quoted in piasters, not in strings, and the value of silver fell more than the value of rice. In fact, this was a period of general price increases due largely to expanded quantities of monetary gold and silver, which caused a greater relative reduction in the value of these commodities and therefore a general increase in price because prices were quoted in terms of the rare metals, gold and silver. This relationship is summarized frequently under the term "quantity theory of money."

An experiment attempted by the French in 1902 is of interest as an illustration of the monetary conservatism of the Vietnamese people at that time. A commission, established for the purpose, decided to mint a zinc coin worth 1/600 of a piaster which would eliminate the independent fluctuation of the sapek by tying it to the silver piaster. Each one of the new sapeks was to be exchangeable for five of the old sapeks. The new sapeks under this arrangement became legal tender. The arrangement seemed to be logical, practical, and workable; but the planners had neglected to consult the people. The population refused to accept the new coin, and it was withdrawn in 1914.

Despite this original failure to unify the money of Viet-Nam, the piaster gradually replaced the sapek; and the sapek became a coin used only in the hinterland. Later in 1947, when this area came under the control of the Viet Minh government, the Viet Minh ordered and enforced the withdrawal of the bronze sapek (the zinc sapek had disappeared about 1925).

As Viet-Nam and most of its neighbors moved on to the silver standard, while France was on a bimetallic standard and later a gold standard, it became necessary for France to provide a silver coin to meet the needs of Viet-Nam. France's first effort along this line was to establish the 5-franc *ecu* at 90/100 of the piaster. This failed because the *ecu* was overvalued. Later in 1885 the Banque de l'Indochine established the French trade dollar with the same exchange value as the Mexican dollar. It was in 1885 that Viet-Nam is considered to have gone on the silver standard on which she was to stay until 1915 (World War I) or perhaps until 1930, when Viet-Nam went on the gold bullion standard that continued until 1936.

It is reported that paper currency, at least in modern times, entered Viet-Nam by the back door on 7 December 1919. Certainly one is justified in saying that this was as evil a day as the 20-year-later bombing of Pearl Harbor on another December 7th. The paper currency was issued through the exchange commission as a method of avoiding further loss of gold reserves by France. The scheme provided that the Banque de l'Indochine turn over its banknotes to Vietnamese exporters equal to 20 per cent of their exports and turn over the foreign exchange equal to this value of banknotes to the Governor General of Viet-Nam. The BIC continued to provide the fiduciary issue of Viet-Nam until 1952.

It was perhaps unfortunate that Viet-Nam went on the gold bullion standard—gold did not circulate and the minimum amount redeemable in gold was 50,000 piasters. The gold weight of the piaster was set at 695 milligrams which was equal to 10 francs in 1930, for it was the beginning of the great depression and the general departure from the gold standard of the trading nations of the world. France and Viet-Nam stayed on the gold standard longer than most nations, and this had a particularly unfortunate effect on Viet-Nam, for it caused the domestic prices of its exports to be seriously depressed.

On 26 December 1945, the piaster was revalued in relation to the French franc. Both currencies had depreciated seriously in terms of the American dollar; but the French franc was assumed to have fallen more rapidly than the piaster, so the new franc-piaster rate was set at 17 to 1. This estimate turned out to be incorrect, and it was not long before the black market rate was 8 to 1. In recognition of this, a new official rate of the French franc to the piaster was set on 11 May 1953. It is this rate of 10 francs to 1 piaster which is still in effect, although the rate on the limited-access free market is about 5 to 1.

Now that Viet-Nam again has control over its monetary system, I hope that the flow of international events will permit the establishment of a money system which truly meets the peculiar needs of Viet-Nam in as effective a manner as did the sapek in the former days of independence.

Part V

ROLE OF
AN ECONOMIC ADVISOR

Role of an Economic Development Council

A portion of the problem of economic development has been the method of organization and administration. Professor Lindholm in his role as Coordinator of a university advisory group to Korea spoke on this problem in Seoul in June 1960. This speech is published in "A Report on the University of Oregon Advisory Mission to the Korean Economic Development Council, 1959-1961," University of Oregon Press in Eugene.

When I was here for a thirty-day period eighteen months ago, you and your predecessors very generously set aside time to discuss with me what might be done under the ROK legislation establishing an Economic Development Council. After about a year of accomplishment and experience of EDC and the ancillary functions of the University of Oregon Advisory Group, I shall be asking for some of your time again during the next three-week period.

To facilitate the development of these conversations and in order to pin-point common areas of interest and concern, I intend this evening to summarize very briefly my experience when here in December of 1958; the resulting key provisions that were included in the operational plan; the resulting contract arrangement; the very considerable accomplishment; and the goals for the next twelve months.

During my original visit, each time I asked the executive with whom I was talking what he thought EDC and its university advisors could accomplish, the result was an outpouring of suggestions and desires. Each of these—which varied from supervising the black market to giving the college student a realistic picture of how a viable production and distribution system must function—was carefully written down.

The review of the proposals indicated that basically EDC and its university advisors were seen as a group that could solve all of the old hoary problems that had been vexing all the groups engaged in efforts aimed at developing a viable and democratic economy in Korea.

These interviews made several points crystal clear:

1. The people charged with the development of an economically viable and democratic Korea had many problems they would like to have solved by some miracle—in this aspect they were somewhat like the natives of the South Pacific, and the EDC was the ship to appear over the horizon to solve all problems.

2. Nobody was willing or thought it feasible to give EDC the dictatorial powers it would need to face these problem-solving proposals.

3. Nobody had thought about all the various elements existing in the local situation which should necessarily set the character of EDC and the scope of its activities.

4. It was up to the Public Administration Division, the economic advisor to USOM, and myself to do the best possible to assign a useful role to the EDC university advisory group.

Basically what was evolved can be summarized in two sentences taken from the Operational Plan, Appendix B, of the contract:

Establish annual development programs based on policies and priorities developed from research.

It is expected that each year the EDC would publish a book made up of special studies of particular aspects of the Korean economy and a summary and analysis of the economy during the previous year.

These two basic sentences of the project description clearly point out the fundamental decision that was made as to the boundaries of the project—the project would not solve problems, but would attempt to provide information through research that would be useful to officials responsible for various vital programs.

The decision to root the function of EDC in research activities arose from two rather fundamental realizations:

1. That the effectiveness of all activities of responsible Korean and American officials was seriously hampered by lack of information.

2. That only if the powers of EDC and the university advisory group were substantially expanded would it be possible to go beyond "establishing annual development programs."

A word of explanation of this second fundamental realization is in order. The annual development programs that could be established under the allocation of power possessed by EDC would necessarily amount to not much more (but remember that this would be a great improvement) than a systematic presentation of all operating agency plans, a forecast of future private economic trends, and a research-based analysis of the priorities indicated. A planning agency to go beyond the limits established for EDC and the university advisory group must be established as a very powerful agency indeed. This expansion has been attempted in democratic countries, maybe most notably in India. But even where attempted, the success has not been marked; and in actual practice the scope has usually been limited to the control of the budget and labor material requirements of selected products.

The success of the work of EDC and its university advisory group has been particularly bright during this first year. For the first time in the history of Korea, an integrated summary or plan of production and distribution was developed. This plan so faithfully represented the aims of the Korean operating agencies and the forecast was so well grounded that it was used as the basis for the development of the national budget—certainly an indication of thorough and useful work.

An economic plan is made up of many parts, and the outcome will be as forecast only if the functioning of each part takes place. The next step after an original plan has been completed is to examine certain parts of the functioning economy to determine if that part can do better, or perhaps why it is doing so badly. This determination can be done only by advancing research portions of the program.

The stage of activity for EDC and its university advisors during the next twelve months is the realization and analysis of essential supports and obstacles to economic growth. The operation plan of the contract envisages that in time EDC will remove itself from the actual organization and gathering of research and instead will perform a purely analytical and integrative function. In the words of Appendix B:

> It is hoped and expected that in the long run, the EDC will become the channel through which specialized studies of various public and private agencies are evaluated for accuracy and soundness of conception, and also the agency which integrates these specialized bits and pieces of information into a picture of the functioning of the Korean economy.

The semi-annual report of the university advisory group covering the period 15 September 1959 to 15 March 1960 points out, after noting that an additional four-year program is under consideration by EDC, that:

> The above arrangements for a research program (are) vital if the four-year plan is . . . kept firmly grounded on the reasonable possibilities of achievement.

The operational plan as set down in Appendix B goes beyond research that could be carried out entirely in Korea and provides for "research backstopping" on the campus of the University of Oregon. Here we have an additional opportunity to examine what is recommended to develop the economy of Korea. The University could also give related data to executives in Korea about the experiences of all races, peoples, times, and places.

Work of the University of Oregon Group in Korea

The work of an advisory group is never completed and the lot of the group is never a happy one, as is shown in the following memorandum also published in "A Report on the University of Oregon Advisory Mission to the Korean Economic Development Council, 1959-1961," by the University of Oregon Press in Eugene.

The memorandum was addressed to Dr. Carroll Shaw, who was the United States Mission administration officer directly responsible for coordinating much of the work being carried out by American advisory groups in Korea.

1. Worked out arrangements for moving EDC to a new and suitable office building. The new building was in the process of construction when the move was made.

2. Worked with the best of the personnel assigned to EDC to gain an understanding of the principal directions in which the three-year plan that had been under way since December 1958 was moving.

3. Each member of the Oregon Advisory Group was assigned to particular divisions of EDC. The assignment was based on each advisor's specialization. In this way the direction of the work of EDC divisions was sharpened. In the words of Appendix B of the Operational Plan, "This technical assistance will consist largely of advisory activities wherein the contract staff will sit alongside the EDC and will be concerned with broad and long-run problems of development. The responsibility for the development of policies will rest with the EDC, and the Contractor will not attempt in any way to control the policy direction of the EDC." In addition, the Operational Plan provides for "Advising on research and planning procedures and giving assistance to EDC in carrying forward its projects."

4. The OAG found EDC to be very loosely organized and that many members of the staff were not qualified to advance useful planning activities. Desirable re-organization plans were discussed with EDC in February and again in June. The lapse of time between the two periods of rather formal organization suggestions arose because of the "revolution." In the words of Appendix B, Operational Plan, "As requested, the Contractor will advise on matters of organization, staffing and internal procedures."

5. The School of Business Administration organized an all-university advisory group to OAG under the chairmanship of Professor Beal. This group developed campus research interests and gave advice to "Chief of Party" and "Campus Co-ordinator" when requested.

6. OAG employed several technically trained Koreans to act as translators and as sources of information. In the words of Appendix B, Operational Plan, "Korean staff members used overseas by Contractor will be employed by EDC in consultation with the Chief of Party."

7. OAG prepared with the assistance of Korean staff personnel a summary of the first three-year plan of EDC. This summary has been widely circulated among interested American groups.

8. OAG developed a cooperative translation effort in EDC to make available a translation of the complete three-year plan. Most of this work has now been completed and a copy has been given to PA of USOM/Korea, as provided in Operational Plan, Appendix B, Part VI, "(2) assisting in the development of publications."

9. OAG held a series of seminars and informal conferences with EDC, as provided in Operational Plan, Appendix B, Part VI, "(4) presenting scholarly papers discussing problems facing EDC," and "(7) training and developing EDC staff."

10. OAG carried out several series of meetings with USOM/Korea staff specialists and University of Oregon campus specialists in order to assist EDC in their efforts to work out fundamental studies in areas such as currency stability, foreign trade trends, agri-business development, power requirements, and government business management efficiency, as provided in Operational Plan, Appendix B, Part VI, "(3) working with EDC, USOM and on-campus specialists in developing fundamental studies."

11. Efforts of OAG to encourage inter-ministerial cooperation have not as yet resulted in concrete actions.

12. From June through August OAG will have as an advisor in Korea Professor Paul Simpson, an econometrician and statistician. He

is analyzing some aspects of Korean statistical publications and providing instruction in the general area of mathematical economics.

13. From 17 June to 8 July 1960, Dean Lindholm worked with many groups of the ROK government and USOM/Korea in a follow-up of his visit in December 1958. The principal aim of these activities has been to complete arrangements for greater integration of economic planning functions in Korea.

14. Since 20 June 1960, OAG has included Dr. Forrest Pitts, an economic geographer with considerable practical experience in increasing rural productivity in the Orient.

Evaluation of EDC

EDC personnel were brought together about two years ago. Many of the appointments were political and, in addition, professional members did not enjoy the job protection available to persons doing similar types of work in the regular government ministries. The overthrow of the dominance of the Liberal Party has resulted in a very serious drop in the morale of the EDC staff, and many members have discontinued their association with EDC. Therefore, to a considerable extent EDC will have to be restaffed and re-organized during the next several months. At this time EDC is only partially functional. The time is appropriate to reconsider the desirability of re-establishing EDC in the form that existed in 1959.

THE SCHOOL OF
GOLDEN ANNIVERSARY YEAR
50
1914 - 1964
UNIVERSITY OF OREGON
BUSINESS ADMINISTRATION